Viking Age York and the north

**Edited by
R A Hall**

Research Report No 27

1978
The Council for British Archaeology

1

© Authors and Council for British Archaeology 1978

ISBN 0 900312 65 3

Designed by Allan Cooper FSIA and Valerie Horsler

Published by
The Council for British Archaeology
112 Kennington Road
London SE11 6RE

Reprinted 1982 by
York Archaeological Trust for
Excavation and Research Ltd
47 Aldwark
York YO1 2BX

Printed at Tomes of Leamington

Contents

Contributors

P V Addyman	York Archaeological Trust
D A Brinklow	York Archaeological Trust
Michael Dolley	Modern History Department, The Queen's University of Belfast
J R A Greig	Archaeological Laboratory, University of Birmingham
R A Hall	York Archaeological Trust
H K Kenward	Environmental Archaeology Unit, University of York
A King	Ingleborough Community Centre
J T Lang	Neville's Cross College, Durham
Arthur MacGregor	York Archaeological Trust
D J Rackham	Archaeology Department, University of Durham
P H Sawyer	Modern History Department, University of Leeds
Alfred P Smyth	Keynes College, University of Kent
P J Spencer	Environmental Archaeology Unit, University of York
D Williams	Environmental Archaeology Unit, University of York

Preface

The majority of the papers in this volume were delivered at the Fourth York Archaeological Weekend, held on 19-21 November 1976, whose theme was 'Viking York and the North'. The amount of interest they engendered has prompted their publication, and in the interim their authors have had the opportunity to make whatever changes they felt desirable for the transition from lecture to printed page. There has been no attempt to standardize authors' choices of personal name forms.

Two contributors to the conference have already had the substance of their papers published elsewhere. Parts of Dr A P Smyth's lecture 'New light on the Scandinavian kings of York' are incorporated in his book *Scandinavian York and Dublin, I* (Dublin 1975) and in an article 'The *black* foreigners of York and the *white* foreigners of Dublin' in *Saga book of the Viking Society for Northern research* volume 19, parts 2-3 (1975-6), 101-17. He has nevertheless written a brief summary of York's history in this period for this volume. An impression of Mr B Ó Ríordáin's lecture 'The analogue: pre-Norman Dublin' can be gained

from his two papers 'Excavations at High Street and Winetavern Street, Dublin' in *Medieval Archaeology* 15, (1971), 73-85, and 'The High Street excavations' in *Proceedings of the Seventh Viking Congress,* edited by B Almqvist and D Greene (Dublin 1976), 135-40. However, additional papers on commercial/industrial and environmental aspects of Anglo-Scandinavian York have been included, and Mr P V Addyman's introductory lecture to the conference, which dealt with the recent work of the York Archaeological Trust in general, has been replaced by an introduction to the theme of the conference and this publication.

I should like to take this opportunity to acknowledge the work of Mr J T Gleave, of the Special Courses Division, University of Leeds, in organizing the 1976 conference, and to thank Mr P V Addyman, Mrs Valerie Black, and Mrs Valerie Horsler for their help and comment in the preparation of the papers for press.

R A Hall, June 1977

Introduction

P V Addyman

The activities of the Vikings in England have always been an attractive subject for study, but also an intractable one. Contemporary and later historical sources make it evident enough that the various Scandinavian raids of the 8th and 9th centuries, and the settlements of the 9th, 10th, and 11th, fundamentally affected the character of English life, society, and institutions. For northern England, and especially for Yorkshire, the all-pervasiveness of Scandinavian influence is particularly clear. It is seen in the character and nomenclature of medieval institutions; in both personal and place names and dialect forms; from the numismatic evidence; in archaeological finds of the period; and in artistic influences, especially on sculpture. That the evidence exists is common ground between scholars. How much of each kind there may be has not always been certain, and several great systematic studies have been undertaken during the last half century to establish this. What conclusion can be drawn from the evidence, however, is still very much a matter of contention. Enough progress has been made with the great corpora, and sufficient new evidence has recently been recovered or recognized, to make a review of Scandinavian influence on Yorkshire worthwhile. The papers in this volume go some way to providing such a review.

The task of assembling the evidence, often disparate and sometimes ambiguous, began early in the century with the work of W G Collingwood. His main interests included two of the subjects under discussion in this volume: the archaeological evidence and the sculpture. His first gathering of the archaeological material (Collingwood 1907a) was followed by the magisterial catalogue of British Viking antiquities published under the editorship of Haakon Shetelig (1940), though even this leaves many articles unillustrated and incompletely evaluated. For York, the source of most of the Viking finds in Yorkshire, the evidence up to 1959 was reviewed by Waterman (1959) in a model study of the relevant museum collections. This is impressively brought up to date in Arthur MacGregor's paper below. For areas outside York the modern detailed corpus remains to be written though there are useful specific studies, such as that by D M Wilson of carpenters' tools (Wilson 1968a).

Collingwood's main interest was sculpture. His own work, published in a series of articles and culminating in *Northumbrian Crosses of the pre-Norman Age* (1927) provided a convenient compendium of the then-known material. Collingwood's conclusions and interpretations have been challenged, emended, or supplemented several times, notably by Sir Thomas Kendrick (1949) and in a work by Pattison (1973) establishing the cultural importance of the York School. Only in recent years, however, has work started on a new corpus, including sculpture discovered since Collingwood's day and all the extant pieces, recorded to a uniform standard. The support of the British Academy for this imaginative project, now in progress under the leadership of Professor Rosemary Cramp, has led to the emergence of a powerful Durham school of students of

early sculpture. J T Lang's essay below, on the Yorkshire material of the Anglo-Scandinavian period, shows the kind of results to be expected from this work. His conclusions have a fundamental importance both for the date and character of the sculpture itself, but even more importantly for its interpretation as an indicator of the character and extent of the Scandinavian settlement. He has, moreover, had the advantage of access to the newly discovered York Minster sculptures which prove, as might have been expected, to be the fount of artistic influence in the region (Lang 1976; 1977).

The past two decades have seen a virtual revolution in our understanding of the Anglo-Saxon coinage. For northern England in the Viking period progress has come in two ways. Firstly, publication of corpora of the coins themselves, through the British Academy's *Sylloge of Coins of the British Isles*, has made the evidence universally available. For York, for instance, it is particularly useful to have Miss E J E Pirie's *Coins in Yorkshire Collections* (1975) which contains many of the local finds, and makes it possible to calculate the incidence of coin loss and hoard concealment in York (Fig 1). Secondly, Professor Michael Dolley's study of the Hiberno-Norse coinage (1966a) took the study of the Viking output itself to a new stage of understanding. His paper below, with characteristic vigour and perception, brings even greater precision to the York series, incidentally crystallizing some hitherto rather fluid history. For the York mint we now await two studies. The first is the massive study of the *sceatta* and *styca* series which will make clear the mint's history in the pre-Viking phase, working from the sound basis established by Lyon (1957). This study, now beginning under the guidance of Miss Pirie, in cooperation with the Department of Nuclear Physics, University of Bradford, will require both typological, metrological, and analytical work on the vast series. The second is a corpus of the whole product of the York mint, along the lines defined for us by Mossop's study of the Lincoln mint (1970) and now being provided by the Winchester Research Unit for the Winchester and Southampton mints.

Since 1972, when the Council for British Archaeology's Urban Research Committee began to promote urban rescue archaeology in the face of destruction caused by central renewal projects in many English towns (Heighway 1972), there has been a transformation in our understanding of the layout and character of the Anglo-Saxon town. In the Danelaw progress has primarily come at Lincoln and York. The emergence of an important industrial and commercial community along Flaxengate, Lincoln, and indeed the establishment and character of the street itself, have been meticulously recorded in Miss Christina Colyer's hugely productive excavations. Evidently some of the premises were jewellers' and metalworkers' craft shops, and the work will be of paramount importance for Anglo-Scandinavian archaeology. At York Mr Hall's excavations of tenements running back from Coppergate have provided similar evidence, but for different crafts, amber working

1

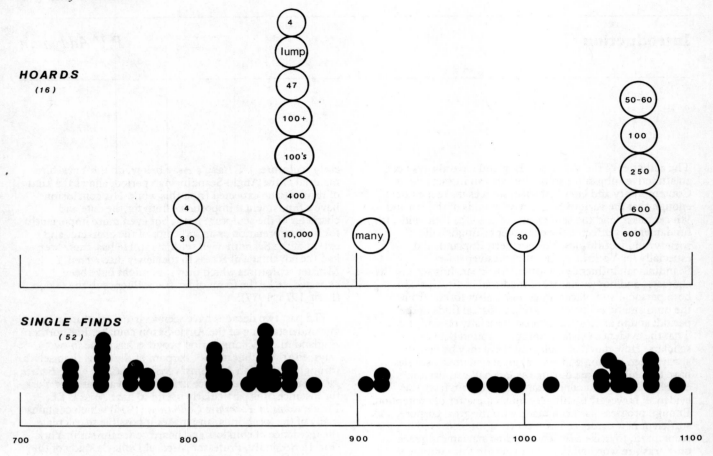

Fig 1   *Incidence of finds of single coins and hoards in York, AD 700-1100*

and wood turning. Six years of continuous excavation and observation by the York Archaeological Trust have, moreover, made possible both the rejection of older hypotheses about the topography and growth of the Anglo-Scandinavian town, and the proposal of new ones. The character of various areas of the town is also beginning to clarify, and it is salutary to consider how much Mr Hall's survey below adds to knowledge of the city. It reminds one how much must have been lost in those post-war years when York was archaeologically dead except for the study of its Roman levels.

The results from the York and Lincoln excavations are something at least to set beside the wealth of evidence from Viking Dublin, and from the Scandinavian towns which were trading partners at the time. Those who attended the conference at York were privileged to hear an account of the Dublin work from Mr Ó Ríordáin, but this is not included here as it has been printed elsewhere (1976).

The greatest lacuna in studies of the Scandinavian settlement of England has always been the complete absence of archaeological evidence of the settlements themselves. Many clearly must lie under modern villages, and Professor Sawyer presents below a stimulating hypothesis about the extent of pre-Viking settlement, and the relationship of Viking settlement to the earlier pattern. It is, moreover, notoriously difficult to detect ethnic traits in the simple occupation material normally found on rural settlements. It is all the more encouraging for the future development of the subject, therefore, that such a clear picture of the layout and way of life on an upland farm of the 9th century has emerged in Mr A King's

excavations at Gauber Pasture, Ribblehead. It seems likely that one day Mr King will lead us to other such farms in the Craven area; but his work should provide a stimulus to settlement archaeology in the whole of the region. As coordinated studies begin, such as are being undertaken as part of the Royal Commission on Historical Monument's investigations on the Yorkshire Wolds, the true role of the Scandinavian settler in the rural landscape should become evident.

The Golden Age of environmental archaeology, it has been said, lies in the future; but the collaborative work of several scholars investigating the environment of early York suggests that it may not be far off. Quite new insights into the natural resources of the region, and their exploitation, have come from the first researches of the new Environmental Archaeology Unit at the University of York. More, it seems, can be learned about social conditions, economic factors, and indeed even climate from the very soils themselves on some at least of our archaeological sites. The existence of the evidence was hardly suspected until recently, and its potential is only now being realized. The first fruits of this particular natural harvest are gathered here.

The fact-finding traditions evident above in various fields of 20th century Anglo-Scandinavian scholarship have also emerged in onomastics. For the place names of York and Yorkshire there is now a corpus in the volumes of the English Place Name Society prepared under the late Professor A H Smith, and a thorough interpretative survey in Dr Fellows Jensen's important book (1972). If there was a gap in the York conference it lay in the absence of a paper on the place name evidence; but of all the categories of source material for the period this is by now the one most readily, completely, and dependably available in print.

More conventional historical sources, too, have responded recently to assembly and analysis. The results of Dr Smyth's work are already in part available (1975) and a fuller treatment of his York paper will shortly be published elsewhere. Another brilliant and provoking paper, also taking the historical evidence as its starting point, was presented to the York conference by Professor Sawyer,

and it is printed here. The two papers between them provided many talking points at the conference; in particular, perhaps, Professor Sawyer's thesis of minimal Scandinavian settlement caused fresh thought in other disciplines. They demonstrated, if ever demonstration was needed, that much still lies in the more or less familiar historical sources. Indeed in all the fields of scholarship represented within this volume it is clear that scholars of calibre are at work; that the evidence now assembled is responding to analysis; and that the intransigence of the subject is beginning to crumble.

Some sources for the history of Viking Northumbria

P H Sawyer

The sources for the history of Northumbria in the two centuries between the Viking and Norman Conquests are not voluminous and most are only preserved in later, often incomplete, copies. Some other parts of England are far better provided with contemporary material, and in Northumbria itself there is a striking contrast between the documentary poverty of this period and the rich literary remains of the age of Bede or the magnificent collections of 12th and 13th century charters preserved in the archives of post-Conquest religious houses. There is, nevertheless, a great variety of source material for Viking Northumbria, far too great to be surveyed in one paper, and it is fortunate that the archaeological and numismatic evidence can safely be left to others at this conference, making it possible to limit this contribution to written sources and linguistic evidence.

Most of the manuscript evidence for Viking Northumbria was produced and preserved by two religious houses, the cathedral church of St Peter at York and the community of St Cuthbert which moved, by several stages, from its original home on Lindisfarne to Durham. These were not the only religious communities in Northumbria at that time; the shrines of St John at Beverley and of St Wilfrid at Ripon were visited by Athelstan, probably in 934 (Thompson 1935, 97; Stenton 1970, 342), and Ripon appears to have survived or recovered from its destruction by King Eadred in 948 for it served as a temporary resting place for St Cuthbert in 995 (Thompson 1935, 97-9). Other religious communities are mentioned from time to time; there was an abbey at Carlisle late in the 9th century (*Historia*, c 13) and an abbey at Heversham, in Westmorland, survived until the early years of the 10th century when its abbot, Tilred, crossed the Pennines, probably fleeing like others at that time from Viking invaders of the north-west (*Historia*, c 21). Tilred became abbot of Norham on the Tweed, a community that housed the relics of St Cuthbert for some time in the 9th century, and later

in that century the same relics were for a short while at the otherwise unknown abbey, possibly a double monastery, of Crayke, about 12 miles north of York (*Historia*, c 20; Whitelock 1955, 93). Whether or not communities left any trace did not depend on their success in serving the spiritual and secular needs of their localities, but on their successors, if any, in the 12th and later centuries. If, thanks to physical destruction or a more gradual process of secularization, a community failed to survive into that relatively more literate age, it is unlikely to have left many recognizable traces, and those communities that did survive so long must have appeared very strange to 12th century monks or canons, who can hardly be blamed for discarding their old service books and neglecting to preserve the memory of their unreformed predecessors. To the post-Conquest reformers the North was indeed a monastic desert (Baker 1970).

These communities were religious and the books they treasured most, and that have been preserved best, despite the misfortunes of time, were those needed for the proper performance of their liturgical functions; copies of the Gospels, the Bible, service books, calendars, and material needed to keep the liturgical year correctly. Historians have, however, naturally tended to pay particular attention to the rather more secular writings produced in or for these communities, notably the chronicles or annals recording events that affected their life, and the charters that were the title-deeds of their estates. The historian of Viking Northumbria suffers from the disadvantage that no contemporary manuscripts of any pre-Conquest Northumbrian chronicle or charter has survived. Fortunately some post-Conquest writers did make use of Northumbrian chronicles in compiling their accounts of the past and it is therefore possible to recover some of the material that has been lost. One version of the *Anglo-Saxon Chronicle*, commonly referred to as the D version, was written towards the end of the 11th century and its compiler drew heavily on annals from York which, for the period to 1031, were also incorporated in the E version, copied at Peterborough early in the 12th century (Whitelock 1961, xiv-xvii). Another set of 9th and 10th century annals was used by the compiler of the collection known as the *Historia Regum* and attributed to Symeon of Durham (Whitelock 1955, 118, 251-4; Hunter Blair 1963; Baker 1975), and a century later a St Albans chronicler, Roger of Wendover, used the same, or a very similar source (Whitelock 1955, 255-8). These annals show a particular interest in the affairs of St Cuthbert's community and the probability that they derived from that house is strengthened by their description of kings in York as ruling 'beyond the Tyne' (Whitelock 1955, 251). Another important, if rather neglected, source that certainly came from that community is the *Historia de Sancto Cuthberto* which is not so much a chronicle as an account of the Patrimony of St Cuthbert (Craster 1954). This text appears to have been compiled originally in the mid 10th century and to have ended with an account of King Edmund's visit to the shrine in 945. It survives in three medieval manuscripts, the earliest in a late 11th century hand, by which time the text had been enlarged both by the addition of some account of grants made early in the 11th century (cc 29-32) and also by an interpolation describing a miraculous visitation in which St Cuthbert assured King Alfred of victory against the Danes in the critical battle of Edington in 878 (cc 14-19 except the last sentence).

The charter evidence for Viking Northumbria is unsatisfactory; only thirteen pre-Conquest charters, or related documents such as wills or writs, granting estates in Northumbria are known and they are only preserved in later copies (Sawyer 1968, nos 68, 407, 667, 681, 712, 716, 968, 1067, 1159, 1160, 1243, 1493, 1536; Hart 1975, 117-30). In making a copy mistakes could easily occur, and it was always possible in the process to alter a text deliberately in order to enlarge the estate, for example by changing the boundary clause, or to increase the privilege that had been conferred. It was also possible to fabricate whole charters and when this was done on the basis of authentic but now lost texts, the detection of forgery can be very difficult. When charters survive in their original form the script serves as a test of the period of composition, and interpolations or alterations can be detected, but if texts are known only in later copies there is often some uncertainty about their interpretation. The charter evidence for pre-Conquest Northumbria is, although slight and not well preserved, of great value. The kind of information that can be gleaned and some of the problems of interpretation are well illustrated by the charter of King Athelstan granting Amounderness to Archbishop Wulfstan and the church of York (Sawyer 1968, no 407; Whitelock 1955, no 104). It has a boundary clause defining the territory being granted which Athelstan is said to have bought 'with no little money of my own', presumably from the Vikings who had seized it and given it its Scandinavian name, the *ness*, or headland, of Agmundr. This charter was copied twice into a 14th century register at York and its authenticity has been doubted for several reasons, including a serious discrepancy in the dating clause in which the incarnation date 930 does not agree with other indications which are for 934. According to the text the grant was made 'at the time I constituted Wulfstan archbishop', that is in 930, but as Professor Whitelock has pointed out, the clause about Wulfstan's accession could be a later insertion or the grant could have been made in 930 and the charter not drawn up until Athelstan visited Northumbria in 934. Professor Whitelock has put forward very good reasons for accepting this as an authentic charter granted at Nottingham on

7 June 934 as Athelstan made his way to Scotland. The witness-list includes both archbishops, three Welsh sub-kings, sixteen bishops, seven ealdormen with English names, six earls with the Scandinavian names Ragnald, Ivar, Hadder, Scule, Thurferth and Halfden, and a further 24 men with English names, eleven of whom are described as king's thegns. An original charter issued at Winchester ten days earlier, on 28 May (Sawyer 1968, no 425), has an almost identical witness-list, which suggests that we probably have here a record of the leading members of Athelstan's retinue on his Scottish campaign that year.

The fact that witness-lists show who was attending the king from time to time means that we are not limited to the handful of charters concerning Northumbrian estates; it is other texts that show the rare attendance of the bishops of Chester-le-Street, or the fact that Archbishop Wulfstan was absent from the English king's court from 934 to 942, an absence that appears to be particularly significant in the light of other evidence that Wulfstan was less than wholehearted in his support of the English kings' authority in Northumbria (Whitelock 1959, 71-73).

As many Northumbrian charters have been lost we have to rely on summaries or notes, some of which are in fact pre-Conquest, namely those added to the Durham *Liber Vitae* (Sawyer 1968, nos 1659-61), the memoranda about the estates of York made by Oswald after he became archbishop in 972 (Sawyer 1968, no 1453), and the list of York estates that were added to a copy of the Gospels early in the 11th century (Robertson 1956, no 84). For Yorkshire and the area south of the Ribble we have the evidence of Domesday Book but that survey did not extend north of the Tees and the *Historia* is therefore especially valuable, for it makes it possible to study the acquisition and loss of estates by the church of St Cuthbert in some detail. For example, it records that Billingham on Tees was given to St Cuthbert by Bishop Ecgred (830-45) but that it was later seized by Ælle, one of the rivals contending for the Northumbrian kingdom when the Vikings captured York in 866 (*Historia*, cc 9-10). It was later recovered, possibly by Abbot Eadred of Carlisle who recovered several estates for St Cuthbert from the Danish king Guthfrith, who died in 895, and from the Danish army (*Historia*, c 19). Sometime in the pontificate of Cuthheard (900-15) it was leased to Alfred, son of Brihtwulf, who is described as fleeing from the pirates and coming across the mountains towards the west (*Historia*, c 22; Whitelock 1955, 261-2). Soon after this a new Viking leader called Ragnald seized power in York (Smyth 1975, chapter 6) and the *Historia* (c 23) explains that he divided the estates of St Cuthbert between two men, Scula, possibly the man who later attended Athelstan's court, and Olaf Ball (Whitelock 1955, 262). This text therefore shows how complex relations were between the community of St Cuthbert and the Scandinavian invaders, not all of whom were hostile to that church. Indeed, according to the *Historia* (c 13, cf Whitelock 1955, 261) the Viking king Guthfrith owed his election to the intervention of St Cuthbert, and then 'Bishop Eardwulf brought to the army and to the hill the body of St Cuthbert, and over it the king himself and the whole army swore peace and fidelity, for as long as they lived; and they kept this oath well.' In contrast, the *Historia* (c 10) blames native English rulers for the loss of estates. This text is also interesting for the emphasis it places on the buying and selling of land, a series of transactions that should be considered along with other references to the purchase of land, including Athelstan's acquisition of Amounderness; one may also compare Copeland in Cumberland (a name that means 'bought land') which Sir

Frank Stenton suggested was similarly purchased from the Vikings (Stenton 1971, 214). There is also a charter of Athelstan that shows Uhtred, a leading supporter of the West Saxon dynasty, being ordered by Edward the Elder to buy land from the pagans in the Peak District in the first decade of the 10th century (Sawyer 1968, no 397; Sawyer 1975, 31-34). These and other 10th century transactions suggest that one consequence of the conquest of large areas of England by Vikings who had made themselves rich by raiding may have been the creation of a land market of a kind that had not existed earlier. (For changing attitudes to land see Charles-Edwards 1976.)

Religious communities were granted estates and privileges for spiritual reasons; in return their members were expected to intercede on behalf of benefactors. The effectiveness of such intercessions was greatly increased by the power of those saints whose remains were the main treasure, and *raison d'être*, of such communities as St Cuthbert's. To the custodians of his shrine St Cuthbert was a living presence, and demonstrations of his power were well remembered. The *Historia*, for example, reports the fall of Olaf Ball, one of the Scandinavians who had taken the Saint's estates and was described as a son of the devil who was hostile in every way he could be to God and to St Cuthbert. The text continues:

> And thus on a certain day, when full of the unclean spirit he entered raging into the church of the holy confessor, he said in the presence of Bishop Cuthheard and the whole community: 'What can this dead man Cuthbert do against me, when his threats are daily disregarded? I swear by my mighty gods, Thor and Othin, that from this hour I will be a great enemy to all of you.' And when the bishop and the whole congregation knelt before God and St Cuthbert, and besought them for vengeance for these threats, as it is written 'Vengeance is mine and I will repay', this son of the devil turned away with great pride and indignation, wishing to depart. But when he had put one foot outside the threshold, he felt as if iron were deeply fixed in the other foot. With this pain piercing his diabolical heart, he fell, and the devil thrust his sinful soul into hell. And St Cuthbert, as was right, received his land (c 23; translation from Whitelock 1955, 262; cf Colgrave 1950).

Religious communities were, of course, particularly vulnerable to the attacks of Vikings who, being pagans, had no respect for the authority of the saints. When Lindisfarne was attacked in 793, Alcuin expressed particular horror that the pagans had 'desecrated the sanctuaries of God, and poured out the blood of saints around the altar, laid waste the house of our hope, trampled on the bodies of saints in the temple of God, like dung in the street . . . What assurance is there for the churches of Britain, if St Cuthbert, with so great a number of saints, defends not his own?' (Whitelock 1955, 776). The community survived but later sought refuge on the mainland. The story of the removal from the island in 875 and the seven years of wandering until a new home was found at Chester-le-Street is told, briefly, in the *Historia* (c 20) and more elaborately by Symeon of Durham, who also reports that, a century later, the community moved again to its last home at Durham (*Hist Dun Eccl*, II, vi-xiii; III, i-iv; Arnold i, 56-69, 78-84). There are, however, reasons for thinking that the migrations were more complicated. According to the *Historia* (c 9) the bodies of both Cuthbert and King Ceolwulf were removed from Lindisfarne by Ecgred, who was bishop from 830 to 845. He took them to Norham on the Tweed where he also rebuilt the dismantled church of Aidan from

Lindisfarne. This translation of St Cuthbert is confirmed by an important, if neglected, text known as the *List of Saints' Resting Places in England* (Liebermann 1889; Birch 1892, 87-94; Rollason forthcoming). The list was put together in its present form early in the 11th century but the first part was an earlier compilation based on 9th century material recording the situation before the Viking conquests; in this section Ealhmund's resting place is described as *Northweorthig*, not Derby, the name it acquired after the Viking occupation. According to this list, St Cuthbert rested not at Lindisfarne or Chester-le-Street but at *Ubbanford* on the River Tweed, that is at Norham. One of the two versions of this list has an interpolation explaining that St Cuthbert is at Durham, and it was probably a list of this kind that misled William of Malmesbury into thinking that the body remained at *Ubbanford* until the time of King Ethelred (William of Malmesbury, *Gesta Pontificum*, iii, 129, ed Hamilton, 268). The *Historia* does not mention a return to Lindisfarne but simply states, without explanation, that the body was later taken from the island for its seven year journey to Chester-le-Street. It is, of course, possible that the body, and the community, did return to the island in the middle years of the century, but as the Viking assault on England was then growing in intensity such a move seems unlikely. The later tradition that the body was taken from Lindisfarne in 875 is probably due to the importance of the island in the life of Cuthbert, reinforced by the natural desire on the part of later members of the community to minimize the importance of Norham. In his account of Ecgred's pontificate, Symeon of Durham omits any mention of this earlier translation although he does report that Ecgred built a church at Norham in honour of SS Peter and Cuthbert, and transferred the body of Ceolwulf to it (*Hist Dun Eccl*, II, v; Arnold i, 52-3). The feast of the translation of St Cuthbert was already observed in the 9th century when the calendar in Bodleian MS Digby 63 was compiled (Wormald 1934, 1-13). This calendar includes not only the original feast on 20 March, which had been observed from a very early date and occurs in Willibrord's Calendar, written before 721, but also a second feast on 4 September, a date that was later observed as the translation (*Hist Dun Eccl*, III, iv; Arnold i, 82; Wormald 1939, 176). This manuscript cannot be dated more closely than between 867 and 892 (Ker 1957, no 319) and this second feast may therefore commemorate either the original translation to Norham, or the later move to Chester-le-Street.

The manuscript in which this early calendar occurs is one of the most fascinating, and enigmatic, survivals from Viking Northumbria. It is a collection of computistical texts, some taken from Bede's *De Temporum Ratione*, and includes a Paschal table down to the year 892 and a list of indictions for the period 844-899. It is written in English script. According to the colophon on fo 71 the scribe was Rægenboldus *sacerdos*, who describes it as a *Liber de Conputacio*, and asks for the reader's prayers for himself and for Bærninus, probably the man whose *obit* is noted in the calendar under 15 February. The Northumbrian saints whose feasts are noted and distinguished by crosses as being of special significance demonstrate its northern provenance clearly enough: Wilfrid, John of Beverley, and Oswald, in addition to the feasts of Cuthbert, one of which was of high degree. It is unfortunate that erasures in the colophon have probably removed the name of Rægenbold's church, the words *de wentonia* being an addition made *c* 1000 after it reached Winchester. Dr David Dumville, to whom I am indebted for advice on this and other points, has suggested that, as Rægenbold is a Continental Germanic name, he is unlikely to have been the scribe of this manuscript and that the colophon was probably copied from the exemplar by an unnamed English, probably Northumbrian, scribe. This remarkable book shows that in the years Northumbria was suffering Viking raids and conquests, it was possible in at least one Northumbrian church to gather and copy liturgical and chronological material needed for the proper observance of the liturgical year. Other books were also needed and it is not surprising that those rescued from Lindisfarne in the 9th century should include several copies of the Gospels, a commentary on the Psalms, and a Lectionary (Mynors 1939, nos 1-12), and that one of the greatest treasures of Durham was its *Liber Vitae*, a collection of names to be remembered that was begun in the 9th century on the basis of older lists that have not survived (Thompson 1923). Names were added from time to time including even Erik Bloodaxe (Thompson 1923, fo 51ᵛ). Communities not only preserved old books, they also took trouble to acquire others that were needed, and one of the most interesting additions to the resources of St Cuthbert's community is a volume of collects written somewhere in England in the first half of the 10th century (Thompson and Lindelöf 1927; Mynors 1939, no 14; Ker 1957, no 106). Several additions have been made, including four collects for the intercession of St Cuthbert and, in the same handwriting, a note in Old English: 'To the south of Woody Gate at Aclee in Wessex' (that is, Oakley, near Woodyates, Dorset) 'on St Lawrence's mass-day, on Wednesday, for Ælfsige the bishop' (of Chester-le-Street, 968-990) 'in his tent Aldred the provost wrote these four collects, when the moon was five nights old, before tierce.' The date was 10 August in either 970 or 981 and the scribe was probably the man who added an interlinear gloss in English to the book and who also glossed the Lindisfarne Gospels (Ker 1943). The need for such glosses is a reminder of the poor latinity of many 10th century churchmen (Hohler 1975, 71-74), a weakness that is further demonstrated in other additions to this book, doubtless made at Chester-le-Street or Durham, which include a form for blessing milk and honey that makes liturgical nonsense for, as Mr Hohler has pointed out (1975, 72), it incorporates the greater part of the form for blessing an altar-cross. A form of service could, however, be effective without being comprehended, and no doubt must often have sounded most impressive to observers who were even less learned than the clergy.

There was great interest in the saints of Northumbria outside that kingdom. The *List of Saints' Resting Places* was probably compiled in southern England (Rollason forthcoming) but, after SS Alban and Columba, it deals first with Northumbrian shrines; St Cuthbert at *Ubbanford*, St Oswald the king at Bamburgh, St John at Beverley and SS Egbert, Wilfrid, and Wihtburh at Ripon. The reference to Oswald has been expanded by the explanation that his head is with St Cuthbert, his right arm is at Bamburgh, and the rest of his body is in the New Minster at Gloucester. Other evidence shows that St Oswald's relics were taken to Gloucester from Bardney in Lincolnshire in 909 and housed there in the new church built by the Mercian ruler Ethelred and his wife Æthelfleda, King Alfred's daughter (Whitelock 1961, 61; Plummer 1896, ii 157-8). The relics collected in Edward the Elder's great foundation at Winchester, New Minster, show a similar interest in Northumbrian saints for the list (Birch 1892, 147-53) includes Acca of Hexham and Wilfrid as well as Cuthbert who was accorded special respect by being placed third (between St Peter and St Stephen). Later in that century, before 980, Glastonbury acquired relics of other Northumbrian saints, Aidan and Ceolfrith (Hohler 1975,

70). Another indication of West Saxon interest in St Cuthbert is the dedication of the main parish church of Wells to him. Athelstan certainly went out of his way to patronize and encourage Northumbrian cults, especially that of St Cuthbert. His Scottish campaign of 934 gave him an opportunity to visit and make gifts to the shrines of Beverley and Ripon, but it was to St Cuthbert that he made the most magnificent gifts (*Historia*, c 26; Battiscombe 1956). He gave several books including Bede's metrical and prose life of the saint, which survives at Corpus Christi College, Cambridge, MS 183, and some vestments, including an early 10th century stole and maniple that were placed in the shrine and are still preserved at Durham.

There are some signs that West Saxon interest in Northumbrian cults, especially Cuthbert's, began before Athelstan's reign, under Edward the Elder if not Alfred who, according to Asser, made gifts to Northumbrian monasteries (Whitelock 1955, 275). The account in the *Historia* of Cuthbert's visitation to Alfred is an apocryphal interpolation of a familiar kind, the same role being elsewhere assigned to St Neot, and the relics at New Minster in Winchester could have been acquired at any time before the compilation of the list in the early 11th century. A better indication is the occurrence of Cuthbert in the Litany in the service book known as Leofric A, now Bodleian MS Bodley 579 (Warren 1883; Ker 1957, no 315). This book was written in a continental hand shortly before or after the year 900 but Mr Hohler has pointed out (1975, 78) that the text contains several unmistakably English elements and he has very reasonably suggested that it was written in England by one of the foreign clerks who we know were encouraged to come to this country at that time. The Litany forms part of the original compilation (Warren 1883, 210) and includes, besides St Cuthbert, the important Mercian saint Guthlac, and Patrick who, Mr Hohler (1975, 69) has argued, was probably the supposed founder of Glastonbury. Later in the 10th century this manuscript was at Glastonbury, and it may have been originally produced for that church, but whatever its precise location it clearly shows an interest in St Cuthbert very early in that century, if not in the 9th. There were good reasons for such an interest at that time. The Scandinavian conquerors of Northumbria, East Anglia, and eastern Mercia threatened the security of Wessex, a threat made even more serious in 899 by the defection to the Vikings of Alfred's nephew Æthelwold. Part of the West Saxon response was to support and encourage the lord of Bamburgh who ruled the province that had been Bernicia, north of the Scandinavian kingdom of York. St Cuthbert was the most important Bernician saint and the encouragement of his cult was a natural religious counterpart of the West Saxon secular policy. The contemporary interest in SS Oswald and Guthlac suggests that Edward the Elder and his sister used the same technique in dealing with the southern Danelaw. The *List of Saints' Resting Places* shows signs of revision in the 10th century, including the amendment of the entry concerning Oswald, and the fact that it deals first with Northumbrian and Mercian shrines may mean that it was a product of this interest in the saints of Viking England. It is therefore not surprising that after the crushing defeat of the Scandinavians at Tettenhall in 910, a new Viking ruler in York, Ragnald, should have been the enemy of St Cuthbert —he seized the saint's estates—just as he was also the enemy of Ealdred who according to the *Historia* (c 22) was loved by King Edward just as his father, Eadwulf of Bamburgh, had been loved by King Alfred.

The power of the Viking kings of York depended mainly on the Scandinavian warriors who settled in southern Northumbria in the last quarter of the 9th century. The written sources tell us very little about this settlement; the *Anglo-Saxon Chronicle* simply reports that in 876 'Healfdene shared out the land of the Northumbrians and they proceeded to plough and to support themselves'; and twenty years later that another Danish army divided, some of the warriors settling in Northumbria. Modern studies of the subject have had to be based on the linguistic evidence of place and personal names. The Scandinavians certainly left their mark linguistically; their language had a significant effect on the dialects of the areas in which they settled and ultimately on modern English, and because they had distinctive personal names and used their own, generally recognizable, words for places and features of the landscape, they transformed the place names in many parts of England. The interpretation of this evidence has, in the past twenty years, been the subject of a lively debate to which my main contribution has been to suggest that the armies were not very large and that the colonization was the work of a relatively small, but powerful, group of men. While there has been a wide measure of agreement about the size of the armies, most scholars have refused to accept my attempt to reduce the scale of the settlement and have argued instead that the linguistic evidence proves that there must have been a substantial immigration. It has also been argued that, if the armies were small, there must have been a secondary migration of Scandinavian peasants who took advantage of the opportunity offered by the conquests to make new homes in England. I do not wish to continue, or even review, that particular debate here; it has been very fully and fairly treated recently by Dr Gillian Fellows Jensen (1975). This is, however, a good opportunity to point out that the entire discussion has until now been conducted on the assumption that when the Scandinavians began to settle in England there were large areas of vacant land awaiting colonization. The Scandinavian place names have been interpreted as the Viking contribution to the process of internal colonization that was also happening in other parts of England, but cannot there be so easily recognized because late English names cannot be readily distinguished from early ones. This assumption that the settlement of England was far from complete in the 9th century has recently been questioned (Sawyer 1974, 1976a). It has been pointed out that our sources, including Domesday Book and early charters, are poor guides to the history of settlement because they tend to deal not with settlements but with estates, and it can be shown that Domesday Book omits a very large number of settlements that certainly existed when it was compiled, especially those that were outlying parts of estates in wooded or hilly country. Archaeology is showing that many settlements are much older than their names, and there is good historical evidence that the resources of England were fully exploited long before the Vikings came. It is most improbable that the Northumbrians would have left such a rich area as the Yorkshire Wolds or even extensive, if less rewarding, lands in the Vale of York, empty. It is therefore now necessary to reconsider the interpretation of the Scandinavian settlements and to explore the possibility that the Vikings were conquerors rather than colonists. Some places may, of course, have

been abandoned—archaeology cannot prove continuity of settlement—and it is possible that some desertions were due to the Viking attacks, but there is no reason to assume that a very large number of places were vacated in that way; lords may have fled, or been killed, but most peasants would have remained. There is no doubt that the Vikings were farmers; their influence on the dialects and on field names proves that they worked the land, unlike the Normans who hardly affected field names at all. But as the *Anglo-Saxon Chronicle* itself explains that Healfdene's followers ploughed the land and supported themselves there is no need to postulate a peasant migration in the wake of the conquest to explain the Scandinavian field names.

The Scandinavian influence on English place names may therefore be evidence not of expanding settlement but of changing ownership. The Vikings seem to have broken up old estates into newly independent units under their individual lordship. The *thorp* names on the Yorkshire Wolds, for example, are best understood not as new settlements by Scandinavian immigrants or their descendants, but as outlying dependencies of estates that had their centres elsewhere and were detached from those centres by the invaders. If the place names that end in the Scandinavian element *by* were formed in the same way, it would explain why a much larger proportion of them have a personal name as the first element in England than in Denmark. Such a major disruption of the traditional system of landholding would certainly have helped create conditions in which land could be bought and sold.

Another consequence of the Viking conquests was the imposition of a new aristocracy who continued to dominate the region long after they had been forced to accept the overlordship of the English king. That overlordship was made more acceptable because the English did not attempt to displace the local aristocracy. In the middle years of the 10th century English kings were content to be described in charters as rulers 'of the Anglo-Saxons and Northumbrians, of the pagans and the Britons', and Edgar provided in one of his law codes that 'secular rights be in force among the Danes according to as good laws as they can best decide on' (Whitelock 1955, 399, 508). The Scandinavians were even welcomed by some leading Englishmen, including archbishops of York, because they helped preserve the traditional independence of Northumbria from rule by southerners. The English kings did little to break down that spirit of independence (Whitelock 1959). It was the Normans who finally destroyed it by the devastations of 1069 and 1085, devastations that were necessary because, in William's eyes, the northerners could not be trusted, and he feared that they might again welcome a Scandinavian invader who could challenge his authority in his newly conquered kingdom.

Acknowledgements

I should like to thank Mr D W Rollason for allowing me to see his paper in advance of publication. I am also indebted to Dr D N Dumville and Dr A P Smyth for their advice.

The chronology of Northumbrian history in the ninth and tenth centuries

Alfred P Smyth

The task of establishing an exact chronology for the history of Scandinavian York is particularly difficult in view of the almost total lack of contemporary annalistic records coming from within the Northumbrian kingdom in the 9th and 10th centuries. It is true that northern versions of the *Anglo-Saxon Chronicle* survive from this period (Versions D and E) (Whitelock 1955, 111-2) and that part of the *Historia Regum* attributed to Symeon of Durham incorporates earlier and genuine Northumbrian annals, but these sources represent at best a fragmentary survival which is not sufficient to equip us with a complete chronological framework for the northern English kingdom. We must, therefore, turn to outside Northumbria for a fuller picture, and this involves us in a study of West Saxon versions of the *Anglo-Saxon Chronicle* and of Irish annals. In view of the hostility between the York Danes and the West Saxons on the one hand, and the dynastic relationship between the rulers of York and Dublin on the other, it is possible not only to reconstruct the story of York from a close examination of West Saxon and Irish sources, but also to establish an exact chronology by correlating the observations of annalists writing independently of each other on either side of the Irish Sea.

There are, however, some formidable difficulties confronting the researcher who attempts to correlate English and Irish records of the ninth and tenth centuries. The *Anglo-Saxon Chronicle* is a source whose complexities are all too often ignored by writers who are not prepared to take a detailed look at comparable contemporary annalistic material from elsewhere in Dark Age Europe. In the Alfredian period, for instance, and especially from 871 to 899, we are dealing not with a set of annals, but with a record which has been very consciously 'written up' in an environment close to the West Saxon court and one which was preoccupied with the Danish wars to the exclusion of other important information, so crucial for the student of chronology, such as records relating to weather and eclipses. The reign of Athelstan, by way of contrast, is not carefully recorded at all even from the military aspect, and the period from 927 to 943, in particular, constitutes a confused and fragmentary record. In some instances, even what remains from this period in the *Chronicle* cannot represent a strictly contemporary account.

Irish annals survive for the most part in late medieval and early modern manuscripts, but these by and large represent faithful copies of the originals, while later accretions to the texts are conspicuous for both their language and content. The dating of these sources all needs adjustment, and this involves a regular correction within each source so that even the 17th century compilation of the *Four Masters* can shed reliable contemporary information on Northumbrian history[1]. We must always bear in mind, however, that Irish observations on the involvement of Scandinavian Dublin in northern English affairs is even further removed from events in York than those of West Saxon writers. In the 9th and 10th centuries the Dublin Norsemen were an alien group separated from Irish annalists by language, politics, and above all religion.

We have also to bear in mind that for parts of the 9th and 10th centuries the Anglo-Saxon year was reckoned, for some purposes at least, to begin on 24 September (Whitelock 1965, ii, cxl-cxlii), while the Irish year was reckoned from 1 January. This means that events occurring between 24 September and 1 January were recorded under different years by Irish and West Saxon chroniclers, and it is impossible to determine the true year for an English event unless the month (and in some cases the date of the month) is specified. Thus, the death of Athelstan is recorded by the *Annals of Ulster* in 938, which after correction dates the event to 939. But Athelstan's death is recorded by West Saxon chroniclers under 940 in the Anglo-Saxon year, because the king died on 27 October 939. Similarly, the correct date for the martyrdom of King Edmund of East Anglia by Ívarr's York army is 20 November 869 rather than the Anglo-Saxon year 870 as recorded in the *Chronicle*. This dating has a crucial bearing on the identification of Ívarr, the slayer of Edmund, with *Imhar* who sacked Dumbarton later in 870, and who returned to Dublin in 871 (Smyth 1977, 233ff).

The fact that the same Scandinavian dynasty ruled over York and Dublin meant that kings moved frequently from one town to the other, and the accuracy with which Anglo-Saxon and Irish annalists independently followed their movements testifies to the veracity of our sources. No less than eight kings of York were involved in the affairs of Dublin, which means that we have an elaborate record spread over a century involving the careers of kings who constantly crossed and recrossed the Irish Sea. Yet, in not one case did Irish or West Saxon chroniclers err by noting the presence of a particular king in both countries at the same time. A detailed study of the chronology of Irish and Anglo-Saxon sources from this period not only allows us to establish that kings such as Ívarr, Hálfdan, and Sigfrith of York campaigned in Ireland (Smyth 1977, 127ff & 255-70; Smyth 1975, 27-40), but it also allows us to reach more precise conclusions regarding the activities of better-known rulers in the 10th century. Irish sources make it clear, for instance, that Gothfrith's disastrous attempt to succeed his kinsman, Sigtryggr, in York in 927 did not last longer than six months, while they also show that Óláfr Gothfrithsson did not sail for England to fight in the battle of *Brunanburh* until after early August 937 (Smyth 1978, forthcoming). Óláfr Cuarán was expelled from York by King Edmund in 944, but he probably remained in the kingdom of Strathclyde until the following year when Edmund raided that region, for we know from Irish sources that Óláfr did not reach Dublin until 945. Similarly, Óláfr's second reign at York probably began late in 948 rather than in 949 (as recorded by Version E of the *Chronicle*) since he was conspicuously absent from a battle at Dublin in 948 when his cousin Blacaire was slain while defending the Norse city from the Irish.

Finally, it is important to stress that we are in a position to exercise some element of control on the dating methods employed by chroniclers scattered across the British Isles in the Viking Age by reference to contemporary European and Oriental writers. Both Irish and English chroniclers dated the death of King Sigtryggr Cáech of York to 927, and English observers noted the appearance of Northern Lights in that same year. This last phenomenon is associated with sun-spot activity and the appearance of both aurora and sun-spots are vouched for by Frankish and Chinese historians respectively in 927 (Schove 1950, 34-49; Smyth 1978, forthcoming). Irish annalists (who recorded a wealth of information on weather and related phenomena) noted in 945 that the lakes and rivers froze over in a 'great and unusual frost' (Hennessy 1887, 464). A chronicler at St Gallen noted a great snowfall in the same year on 15 March, and these icy European conditions were probably part of the same severe winter experienced earlier in the Middle East in 944 and recorded by such writers as Euthychius of Antioch and the Persian historian, Hamza[2]. In the winter of 961, excessive snowfalls were blamed in Ireland for producing distemper and a cattle plague (Hennessy 1866, 212-4, *sa* 959), while Anglo-Saxon writers noted this 'very great mortality' in the Anglo-Saxon year 962 (Plummer & Earle 1965, 114), or the winter of 961-2 in terms of absolute chronology. Records such as these reassure us that while some individual dates can never be ascertained beyond the accuracy of ±1 year, Irish and West Saxon records, when used in conjunction, nevertheless do provide us with an accurate time-scale for events in Northumbria in what almost amounts to the Viking century 865-956.

Northumbrian chronology 865-956

865	Invasion of East Anglia by the Great Army of Danes.
866	Capture of York by the Great Army on 1 November.
867	Defeat of Northumbrian army in vain attempt to dislodge Danes from York, on 21 March. Death of the Northumbrian kings Osberht and Ælla.
868	Great Army at Nottingham.
869	Great Army returned to York and ravaged Northumbria (868-869).
869-870	Great Army moved from York to East Anglia. Defeat and death of King Edmund of East Anglia at the hands of Ívarr (20 November 869). Danish conquest of East Anglia.
871	Great Army invaded Wessex.
872	Northumbrian revolt against Danish rule. Egbert, the Danish sub-king, and Archbishop Wulfhere of York expelled from the city.
873	Hálfdan with his section of the Great Army marched from London to York, suppressed Northumbrian revolt, and reinstated Archbishop Wulfhere. Ricsige installed as Danish sub-king, in succession to Egbert.
874	King Burgred of Mercia abandoned his kingdom to Great Army of Danes.
875	Hálfdan took the kingdom of Northumbria for himself, while his ally, Guthrum, marched south against King Alfred. Hálfdan wintered on Tyne and attacked Picts and Strathclyde Britons. Bishop Eardwulf and his community abandoned Lindisfarne to Danish marauders, and took with them the body of St Cuthbert. Hálfdan arrived in Dublin and slew its king, Eysteinn Óláfsson.
876	Hálfdan settled his Danish warriors in Vale of York and they turned to the plough.
877	Hálfdan expelled from Tynemouth by his warriors. He sailed against Dublin with a few ships and was slain by Dublin leader, Bárdr, at Strangford Lough.
c 883	Lindisfarne monks resettled at Chester-le-Street.

	Election of Guthfrith as first Christian Danish king of York.
893	Northumbrian Danes joined Hásteinn in his war against King Alfred. A Northumbrian leader, Sigfrith, blockaded Cornish peninsula with fleet of about 80 ships based at Exeter and on the coast of north Devon. Sigfrith sailed from Devon to attack Dublin where he was driven off and pursued back to Northumbria by Dublin king, Sigtryggr Ívarsson.
895	Death of King Guthfrith (24 August) and his burial in York Minster. Death of Archbishop Wulfhere of York. Sigfrith succeeded to the York kingship and issued coins in his own name.
899	Death of Bishop Eardwulf of Lindisfarne (at Chester-le-Street). Death of King Alfred.
900	Archbishop Æthelbald appointed to the See of York. Ealdorman Æthelnoth of Wessex led a West Saxon embassy to York. The atheling, Æthelwold, son of King Æthelred of Wessex, fled from that kingdom then ruled by his cousin, Edward the Elder, and was accepted as king by York Danes. A great disturbance in Northumbria. A Danish king, Knútr, began to issue silver coinage at York either in conjunction with that of King Sigfrith, or in succession to it.
902	Dublin Norsemen expelled by Irish. Colonization of north-west England by Norsemen. Colonization of the Wirral by Hingamund and his Hiberno-Norsemen.
903	Æthelwold slain, leading a Danish coalition against Wessex.
904	Ívarr II, grandson of Ívarr, slain while raiding in Lowland Scotland.
c 905	Clergy of York Minster issued the first series of 'St Peter' ecclesiastical coinage.
907	Chester fortified by the English. Mercians and King Edward built forts along the Mercian border with the Northumbrian Danes (Tamworth, 913; Eddisbury, 914; Runcorn, 915 etc).
909	Army of King Edward invaded Northumbria.
910	Northumbrians invaded Mercia and were defeated at Tettenhall. Their kings, *Eowils* and Hálfdan, slain. English settlers in north-west (such as Abbot Tilred of Heversham and Alfred, son of Brihtwulf) fled eastwards over the Pennines to safety of Wear valley.
c 911	Ragnall, grandson of Ívarr, took York. Restoration of 'St Peter' coinage at York to its full weight. York coinage issued in name of *Raienalt*.
913	Ragnall moved north to Tyne and drove Ealdred, Reeve of Bamborough, from Bernicia.
914	Ragnall's first victory at Corbridge over Ealdred of Bamborough and Constantine, king of Scots. Ragnall settled some followers between the Tees and Wear. Ragnall's army crossed Lowland Scotland, attacked Dumbarton on Clyde and sailed into the Irish Sea. Ragnall victorious over rival Norse fleet led by Bárdr Óttarsson off Isle of Man.
917	Ragnall and Sigtryggr, the grandsons of Ívarr, invaded Ireland.
918	Ragnall left Waterford with Gothfrith and Óttarr, and invaded Lowland Scotland sacking Dunblane.

Ragnall won second victory at Corbridge on Tyne over Bernicians and Scots.
Stamford and Nottingham finally surrendered to Edward the Elder.

919 Ragnall captured York for second time.
Sigtryggr retook Dublin and slew Irish High King, Niall Glúndub, in a battle outside city.

920 Ragnall and other nothern British rulers submitted to King Edward. Death of Ragnall.

921 Sigtryggr II Cáech destroyed Davonport (Cheshire) and succeeded to York kingship.

924 Death of Edward the Elder and succession of Athelstan (925).

926 Treaty between Sigtryggr of York and Athelstan at Tamworth. Marriage of Sigtryggr to Eadgyth, sister of Athelstan.

927 Death of Sigtryggr and brief succession of Gothfrith to York kingship. Athelstan invaded Northumbria and drove out Gothfrith, demolishing Danish fortress at York. Athelstan assumed kingship of Northumbria and concluded treaty with rulers of northern Britain at Dacre. Return of Gothfrith to Dublin.

934 Athelstan visited Chester-le-Street and led expedition against Scotland. Death of Gothfrith, last of grandsons of Ívarr, in Dublin. Óláfr Gothfrithsson succeeded to Dublin kingship.

937 Óláfr Gothfrithsson of Dublin led Scottish and Strathclyde British coalition against Athelstan. Invaders defeated by English at *Brunanburh*.

938 Return of Óláfr Gothfrithsson to Dublin.

939 Death of Athelstan (27 October). Succeeded by his brother, Edmund.
Second invasion of Northumbria and occupation of York by Óláfr Gothfrithsson.

940 Óláfr Gothfrithsson and Archbishop Wulfstan of York overran Danish Mercia. England divided along Watling Street between Edmund and Óláfr. Óláfr now king of Dublin, Northumbria, and Danish Mercia. Marriage of Óláfr to Aldgyth, daughter of an Anglo-Danish *Jarl*.
Óláfr Cuarán Sigtryggsson left Dublin and joined his cousin, Óláfr Gothfrithsson, at York.

941 Death of Óláfr Gothfrithsson after raiding Tyninghame in Lothian. Óláfr Cuarán Sigtryggsson succeeded to the Hiberno-Danish realm at York.

942 Óláfr Cuarán lost control of Danish Mercia to King Edmund.

943 Óláfr Cuarán baptised at Edmund's court, and his cousin, Ragnall Gothfrithsson, later confirmed there.

944 Edmund invaded Northumbria and drove out Óláfr and Ragnall.

945 Edmund invaded Strathclyde and made it tributary to King Malcolm of Scotland. Óláfr Cuarán returned to Dublin and expelled his cousin, Blacaire, from the kingship there.

946 Murder of King Edmund. Succession of his brother, Eadred.

947 Archbishop Wulfstan of York and Northumbrian *witan* submitted to Eadred at Tanshelf, but shortly afterwards accepted Eiríkr Bloodaxe from Norway as their king.

948 Eadred ravaged Ripon and was attacked by the York army, but eventually forced York to reject Eiríkr Bloodaxe.

949 Óláfr Cuarán returned to York. (His second reign at York probably began late in 948.)

952 Óláfr Cuarán expelled from York and Eiríkr Bloodaxe returned for his second reign.
King Eadred seized Archbishop Wulfstan and incarcerated him at *Iudanbyrig*.

953 Óláfr Cuarán campaigning once more in Ireland where he ruled as king of Dublin until 981.

954 Eiríkr Bloodaxe expelled from York, and slain while escaping across Stainmore. King Eadred succeeded to the kingdom of Northumbria. End of Scandinavian rule at York.
Archbishop Wulfstan restored to a bishopric in Dorchester.

955 Death of King Eadred.

956 Death of Archbishop Wulfstan.

Notes

1. The dating of the *Four Masters* requires the regular addition of two years to the date in O'Donovan's printed edition for the period 913 to 977 (*recte* 915 to 979). Dates for before this period are usually five years behind the true year, while dates for the period 980-1018 require the addition of one year (P Walsh, *The Four Masters and their work*, Dublin 1944, 32). The chronology of the *Annals of Ulster* has fallen one year behind the true date in the period 482-1013 (T F O'Rahilly, *Early Irish history and mythology*, Dublin, reprinted 1964, 241-3).

2. Dr D J Schove, St David's College, Beckenham, Kent, has very kindly supplied this information from his forthcoming book, *The spectrum of time*.

Anglo-Scandinavian sculpture in Yorkshire

J T Lang

There are over five hundred fragments of pre-Conquest sculpture in Yorkshire, the largest number in any English county, and they represent only a fraction of the original wealth of carving in the region. Most pieces are fragments from cross shafts and grave-covers, often only a surviving fifth of the total monument, and there are those sculptures which are immured in the walls and foundations of medieval churches, either completely hidden or built in with only one of the four faces displayed. Nothing redeems the Viking reputation more than the Yorkshire carvings, since of the five hundred pieces nearly 80% belong to the Anglo-Scandinavian period (*c* 875-1066) and the mixed population of York and its ridings was responsible for a great flowering of stone sculpture, developed in a succession of local schools, whose art remains distinct both from the styles of the Scandinavian homelands and from neighbouring insular art in Ireland, Man, or even Northumbria north of the Tees.

The reason for the *floruit* was undoubtedly the growing prosperity of York as a commercial centre. Much of the preceding Anglian work is associated with monastic sites and its iconography is thoroughly ecclesiastical, but the 10th century monuments are for the most part funerary sculpture and occasionally their illustrative carving is uncompromisingly secular or even pagan. The patrons of the monuments were probably prosperous land-holders anxious to display their prestige and more than ready to adopt establishment Anglian habits in their graveyards. At the same time, the sculpture tends to suggest that the church continued in some places to act as patron and there is evidence of interaction between the two traditions.

The distribution of the Yorkshire sculpture has been used as an indicator by place-name scholars and those interested in the phases of Scandinavian settlement in northern England (Sawyer 1971, 165), but the practice is a dangerous one. First, as the topography of Yorkshire illustrates (Hall 1976a, 8), stone sculpture's closest connection is with geology, the source of its raw material. There is very little sculpture in the East Riding, for example, primarily because it is made up of chalk and boulder clay, so its few monuments have been imported: North Frodingham has a Millstone Grit cross-head, Barmston a sandstone hogback, and Nunburnholme a limestone shaft. Sculpture is at its most dense where good freestone is readily available, for example round the edges of the Yorkshire Moors and the Cleveland Hills. Conversely, sculpture is sparse in the Vale of Pickering because in the Viking period much of the land was marsh, the old Lake Pickering, and the monuments are confined to islands of Kimmeridge Clay (de Boer 1965, 198 and 207).

Funerary sculpture tells little of where the Anglo-Scandinavian population lived, but the immobility of the stones fixes in a very firm way the location of their dead. The distribution is barely relevant for settlement studies though crucial for understanding burial practices in the period: the cemetery pattern need not necessarily be identical with the settlement pattern and the problems of the Yorkshire graveyards are complex. For example, there is considerable variation, judging from sculptural evidence, in the continued use of existing Anglian monastic burial grounds by the Anglo-Scandinavian population. Two Ryedale monastic cemeteries provide differing situations: Lastingham continued to be used for burials into the early 11th century, while Hackness has only pre-Viking monuments. Sockburn and Stonegrave are known from literary sources to have had Anglian monasteries yet their monuments are exclusively Anglo-Scandinavian. And the two great cemeteries of Whitby Strand are markedly different; the large collection of memorials from the *Streanæshalch* site contains only one Anglo-Scandinavian fragment, while Lythe, at the northern end of the strand, has an abundance of exclusively Viking period stones.

Dots on a distribution map representing sculpture rarely indicate the very wide dating range of the stones, even at a single site. Collingham, a case in point, has fragments of three monuments ranging from the 9th to the 11th centuries; Otley and Lastingham retain pieces from the 8th to the 11th centuries. The sculpture is rarely contemporary with the personages of Halfdan or Ragnall, and cannot be firmly associated with the first phase of any settlement. Indeed, Anglo-Scandinavian sculpture has all too frequently been interpreted far too ethnically. Moreover, the stones are so fragmentary that their distribution may take on a deceptive aspect; new pieces are emerging at the rate of four or five a year and there are still important gaps to be filled, among them the Anglian sculpture of York itself.

It also has to be admitted that the dating of these stones and the establishment of their chronology are far from secure. There is no fixed point, no documentary evidence, and few inscriptions. We have to depend on an art historical approach to stylistic developments based on the eclectic habits of the sculptors. It is often easier to identify the hands of individual sculptors than to determine date or sequence. Only the Kirkdale sundial can be closely dated to the days of King Edward and Earl Tostig (Collingwood 1907b, 344) and the crosses within the church walls—if they are indeed still Orm's walls built from the ground—must pre-date the sundial. Such broad dating is the best we can hope for, but it is possible to postulate a sequence if not a chronology.

Both Johannes Brøndsted (1924, 223-33) and W G Collingwood (1927, 127-36) proposed their own sequences for the Yorkshire sculpture, based on the material then available. The Pickhill hogback and the Clifford Street, York fragment became classic pieces, serving as focal points in the discussion of the origin of insular Jellinge style art (Shetelig 1948, 96; Kendrick 1949, 90, pl LX; Shetelig 1954, 136). Both carvings must now be regarded as provincial and derivative in the light of Mr Derek Phillips's highly important discovery of the late pre-Conquest cemetery under York Minster where the design source of much of the sculpture spread throughout Yorkshire villages has been revealed. The Minster tombstones (and

Plate Ia   Middleton C (photo: Alan Wiper)

Plate Ib   York Minster I (photo: Alan Wiper)

Plate Ic   Collingham (photo: Alan Wiper)

Plate Id   Brompton (photo: J T Lang)

Plate Ie   Kirkleavington (photo: T Middlemas)

Plate If   Kirkby Misperton (photo: J T Lang)

at last we can be sure that the stones are indeed funerary) represent metropolitan fashions that are borrowed and modified in Ryedale, in Allertonshire, and in the Tees Valley, and it is often the modification of the York designs that leads to the consequent stylistic development of Yorkshire sculpture. The most striking feature of the York stones, including the new fragments from the parish churches, is their high quality (Pattison 1973, pls 39, 43, 45-50; Hall 1975, 21-8). Viking period carving can no longer be regarded as inept, a shadow of Anglian excellence. The 10th century sculptors of York promoted original styles and decoration as well as maintaining continuity with the Anglian tradition both in form of monument and in ornament. For this reason the term 'Anglo-Scandinavian' is more precise than 'Viking', and it is fiction to invent notions of English carvers working to the instructions of a Scandinavian patron to explain away Anglian and Classical elements.

The habit of raising stone crosses and carving grave-slabs was already established in Anglian Yorkshire before the Viking influx. There is little or no comparable stone sculpture in Scandinavia, apart from the very distinct Gotland picture stones. Both Northumbria and Ireland enjoyed well-founded sculptural traditions, however, and the Anglo-Scandinavian carvers belong to this insular art development. The Scandinavian features of their work are chiefly ornamental and, with the notable exception of the hogback, the Viking period repertoire perpetuates free standing crosses and slabs. The persistence of Anglian styles is demonstrated in a monument like the complete cross Middleton C (Plate I*a*). Its free arm cross-head, though contemporary with the more popular wheel-head that came from the west, is typically Anglian and it echoes the hammer-head of some late Saxon forms. The decorative scheme laid out above a raised encircling band places the cross in the round shaft derivative sequence whose origins were thoroughly Anglian, though the type appealed strongly even to sculptors as Scandinavian as the Gosforth master (Bailey & Lang 1975). Its decorative panels contain vinescroll, albeit debased, and a brave attempt at complicated interlace. It even retains traces of red lead paint. The most striking example of coexisting Anglian and Scandinavian elements is the York Minster cross-shaft 3 (Pattison 1973, pls 46-7) which has two faces containing contoured profile animals and two other faces with Anglian derived interlace and an ecclesiastical portrait with a dished halo. This conservatism complicates attempts at establishing a stylistic progression, and local idiosyncracies, together with the copying of antique models, render the task yet more difficult.

The most useful key to the sequence lies in the Nunburnholme shaft (Pattison 1973, 209-34, pls 40-1), since there is clear evidence for a series of three sculptors working on the shaft (Plate II*e*). By comparing the styles of the individual hands and the modifications made to the underlying designs, we find some indication of changing tastes (Lang 1977). Mr Ian Pattison has shown that the top of the shaft should be turned through 180°; the resulting Side 4 represents the work of the First Sculptor and probably the current York taste in design during the early 900s. The haloed figure within an arch is a familiar motif in the Yorkshire Anglian series: Otley in the late 8th century, Collingham in the 9th, a tradition that continues through the 10th century shafts at Leeds and York, culminating in the 11th century Evangelist portraits at Newburgh Priory. Its appearance on the Newgate shaft from York alongside Anglo-Scandinavian animal ornament gives the lie to the notion that Viking taste obliterated Anglian classicism. The drapery forms and

modelling of the Nunburnholme saint and the frieze of gripping angels betray Carolingian sources which were already influential in 9th century carving at Easby. The small beast above the figure has much of the Trewhiddle style in its appearance though its jowl relates it to the flat profile animals of the York Minster collection. On such stylistic grounds, a date in the early years of the 10th century can be proposed for the First Sculptor's work.

It was he who mapped out the initial design for the whole shaft, but he never finished his work. A Second Sculptor resumed the carving, employing a flatter technique and using cruder tools. Incapable of cutting the protruding knees of a frontal seated figure, he turned the portraits into profiles. Much of his carving continues the ecclesiastical strain of the initial design, but the portrait of the seated swordsman with his Viking period sword belongs to the secular illustrations of warriors depicted with their weapons that are so common in Anglo-Scandinavian sculpture. The best known are at Middleton (Binns 1956, figs 3, 10, and 11) though they are frequent throughout Ryedale and at Sockburn on the Tees. The Nunburnholme swordsman is perhaps an early indication of the shift from ecclesiastical designs and of the new lay patronage of monuments. We can be sure that the warrior succeeds the saint at Nunburnholme because the original pelleted arris and frame have been drastically cut back on the left of the figure and on the right the primary incised guidelines of the First Sculptor still survive on the unembellished border, still waiting for the chisel. Secondly, the wings and foliate details of the angel frieze are incomplete on the warrior face (Side 1), the angels' fingers have been chopped, and the pelleted frame rejected. Profiles taken of the mouldings above the saint and the warrior show conclusively that the Second Sculptor cut well into his predecessor's levels, leaving a much rougher surface. The second phase of cutting, then, must post-date the early years of the 10th century, though we cannot be sure of the length of the time lag between the two cuttings.

The Second Sculptor was also responsible for introducing linear animal ornament onto the shaft. These columns of fettered beasts may ultimately spring from Anglian inhabited vinescrolls or zoomorphic borders of manuscripts; their immediate origin, however, lies in 9th century Mercian sculpture. They cannot be termed 'Jellinge' beasts as they are far more substantial than the Jelling cup ribbon quadrupeds and have long legs supporting well-proportioned bodies and long arching necks with thrown back heads. There is no contoured outline despite the extended ear and spiral leg joint that prepare the way for the flatter, elongated dragons of the middle of the century. At Gainford on Tees the large Nunburnholme beast has flattened and developed a double outline in addition to its scrolled leg joints, yet there is still some freedom and space in the design. Fashionable embellishment has been superimposed on the Nunburnholme type of design (Haverfield & Greenwell 1899, 98-9). To the east of Nunburnholme, on the shaft from Folkton (now in the Yorkshire Museum, York), their composition is more densely packed and the beasts are in closer proximity (Fig 2 B, C). Anglo-Scandinavian *horror vacui* is apparent, the beasts beginning to take on the role of a repeating rhythmic pattern (Collingwood 1909, 194 and 197; Collingwood 1927, 129, fig 140). The animals are less independent of the total design scheme and their postures are determined by repeating diagonals within the schematized lay-out.

I take the Nunburnholme-Folkton sequence to be a prelude to the splendid entangled and entwined beasts of

Plate IIc   Leeds   (photo: Alan Wiper)

Plate IIb   Middleton A (photo: Alan Wiper)

Plate IIa   Middleton B (photo: Alan Wiper)

Plate IId   Sutton on Derwent (photo: J T Lang)

Plate IIe   Nunburnholme (photo: M Firby)

Plate IIf   Sinnington (photo: J T Lang)

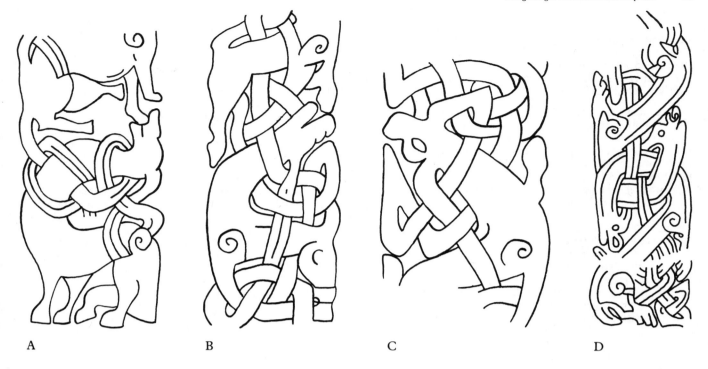

A   B   C   D

Fig 2   Animal ornaments from Anglo-Scandinavian sculpture in Yorkshire: (A) Nunburnholme, (B) and (C) Folkton, (D) York Minster shaft 1

the York Minster cross-shaft 1 (Pattison 1973, pl 47 *a* and *b*) (Plate I*b*). Here the fettered beasts are no longer disposed as almost free standing animals but as zoomorphic interlace. They are still quadrupeds and their arched necks are thrown back even further, but the body and neck are elongated into ribbon beast proportions to form thick interlacing bands that contrast with the extended ears' slender trails. The planning is careful and logical; the cutting deep and lightly modelled. In addition, the decorative details of nose, paws, and joints achieve a highly ornamental appearance far removed from the relative naturalness of the Nunburnholme beasts. The lay-out is characteristic of Yorkshire, however, since it relies on the juxtaposed diagonals seen in the Folkton piece.

The spectacular shaft from Newgate in York (Pattison 1973, pl 43) helps to fix the Nunburnholme shaft in the first half of the 10th century as it copies the modified version of the angel frieze; that is, after the Second Sculptor had confused the foliate fan with the wing (Plate III*a*). Though the Newgate frieze is clumsily executed (remains of paint suggest a more vivid finish), the panels of animal ornament are original, the sculptor having risen above the eclectic habits of his contemporaries, as the Gosforth master did in Cumberland. Close examination of the marks upon the stone reveals the planning by the sculptor: the central axis is marked on the crest of the arch by a small incised line which, when produced, links the point at which the angels' wings meet above with crucial intersections in the animal design below. The wings were marked out with dividers or a punch on a taut string leaving incised arcs and the outlines plotted with a series of small punch

marks. These constructional scratches may have been concealed by a thin wash of gesso, like the St Mary Castlegate wheel-head, and coated with colour.

On one face of the Newgate shaft the animal ornament can easily be mistaken for interlacing strapwork (Pattison 1973, pl 43 *b*) since the ribbon beasts have no legs and small heads. The knot which they form has tangental confronted scrolls with nipping collars at their necks, a feature which relates to Odd's cross on the Isle of Man and thereby associates it with Scandinavian styles of the end of the 10th century. This Manx cross has a further connection with the Yorkshire carvings in its pelleted S-shaped beasts whose snub jowls, disposition, and raised forepaw are closely paralleled in another shaft at Folkton (Collingwood 1911, 258-9) (Fig 3). Typically, the East Riding version is more closely packed and the eye is enriched with a double outline. This beast in turn was copied at the end of the century at Sutton on Derwent where the posture, eye, and foreleg are reproduced. However, the snub jowl has also acquired the nose folds of York animals and while the neck is pelleted the rest of the body is hatched with lines and chevrons in separate zones, in the manner of south-west Mercian beasts (Collingwood 1929, 238-40).

The pedigree of the Yorkshire quadruped can be traced in a sequence from the runic shaft at Collingham (Collingwood 1914, 158) whose animals derive from 9th century sculpture further up the dale at Ilkley (Plate 1*c*). The Collingham shaft could well be a late 9th century piece as its large beast with hanging head and rearing posture is

Anglian enough but its flat treatment, contouring, and extended ear lean to 10th century styles. The confronted beasts below are conceived more as a symmetrical pattern even though the fettering is as yet fairly loose. It should be said, however, that the dating of West Riding pieces is particularly hazardous owing to a much stronger Anglian survival in local taste.

From these discrete beasts we can move to an animal like that on York Minster cross-shaft 2 (Pattison 1973, pl 45 *g*) where the creature is still large, and interlocked only at its neck by a second beast. Its head is now flung back and the body not only fettered but pierced by the extended ear and tail. Similar piercing occurs in a metalwork context from Kaupang where a beast is similarly fettered by its own appendages (Blindheim 1972, 50, fig 26), though it is possible to trace the feature back to Northumbrian manuscripts like the Durham Cassiodorus, B.ii.30, in which the pierced beast appears in the borders of f.81v. The York Minster animal inhabits a long panel which runs the entire length of the shaft, without the divisions or decorative transverse borders of the Collingham shaft. Hence, in returning to the familiar bound dragon of Middleton B (Plate II*a*) we can see that the disposition of the beast is identical with the more coherent York animal and that the single long panel of the shaft is now totally occupied by it (Lang 1973, 21-3, pl IV, 5). This is certainly not the tentative approach to a new style suggested by some commentators (Wilson & Klindt-Jensen 1966, 103-4; Sawyer 1971, 163-6); it is a highly derivative beast and has had provincial decorative details applied to its borrowed form, in the same manner as the Gainford beasts were adapted versions of the Mercian-Nunburnholme type. The looped jaws of the Middleton dragon (it is in fact a quadruped) are a restricted local feature resulting from experimentation in the high stylization of animal forms. The Ryedale dragons are rarely identical in their details despite their recognizably generic character.

The largest shaft fragment at Sinnington, for example, (Plate II*f*) is one of three at the church, all with ribbon quadrupeds disposed in the York S manner but with varied infills of fetter band, scrolls, and in this case a mask (Collingwood 1907b, 387 f) which has a parallel on the 10th century Cammin casket. The jaws of this stone's beast are not quite looped but have horizontal slits which seem to serve a similar function. Villages in Ryedale provide a growing number of both types of jaw, and the well known grave-slab at Levisham (Collingwood 1927, fig 26) shows that the slits may have been associated with the fangs and perhaps later expanded into loops and a threading band (Plate IV*f*).

The Levisham slab has sometimes been cited as an example of 'proto-Ringerike' style, even though this was a style that never appealed in northern England. A single fragment at Otley represents Yorkshire Ringerike (Collingwood 1914, 230 *ii*), a style which was far more influential in Scandinavia and southern England. There is no windswept movement or streamlining about the Levisham beast and its accompanying scrolls have more in common with the Newgate or Odd's cross scrolled features. A comparison with other sculpture from Levisham and Sinnington reveals that the scrolls are a local feature, very restricted in their distribution, the Levisham usage simply transferring the motif to a zoomorphic context. The geographical location of Levisham makes it unlikely that the slab is the influential piece that some would have it (Kendrick 1949, 99). The beast is indeed another derivative one, a cruder copy of elaborate ribbon animals like the one at Gilling West (Collingwood 1907b, 322-3 *d*), where the fetters and body extensions take the form of trailing volutes. The shape of the Gilling shaft, a round shaft derivative type, connects with Middleton C as does its ring-knot on another face, so there is evidence of stylistic borrowing not only between adjacent villages but also between sites fifty miles apart. If we assume that poorer

E   F   G

Fig 3   Animal ornament from (E) Odd's Cross, Braddan, (F) Folkton, (G) Sutton-on-Derwent

Plate IIIa Newgate, York (photo: J T Lang)

Plate IIIb Kirby Hill (photo B Coatsworth)

Plate IIIc Folkton (photo: J T Lang)

Plate IIId Stonegrave (photo: J T Lang)

Plate IIIe Kirkleavington (photo: C D Morris)

Plate IIIf Sinnington (photo: J T Lang)

work is the copy and accomplished work the model, then Gilling would precede Middleton C and the Levisham slab.

A little to the south, on the shaft from Kirkby Misperton (now in the Yorkshire Museum), a sculptor used models from further afield (Brøndsted 1924, 197-8, fig 145). The shaft is shouldered, like those from Whalley and Bolton west of the Pennines, an 11th century type, and its decoration comprises elaborate interlace very reminiscent of manuscript patterns and interlocking beasts with elongated necks and limbs (Plate I*f*). The details about the head are close enough to Ryedale models to suggest some local eclecticism, but the shaft's 11th century date is confirmed by the form and arrangement of the animals which have very close parallels in Ireland both in sculpture and metalwork (Henry 1970, 193, fig 30, *a b c*). However, the Irish influence upon Yorkshire sculpture has perhaps been exaggerated as only one or two pieces display closely paralleled features.

Running alongside this almost baroque animal ornament is a second tradition: the free style, in which horses, stags, dogs, and men are active and recognizable. The two coped faces of the St Denis grave-cover represent the two styles juxtaposed (Collingwood 1909, 165; Pattison 1973, pl 50 *a* and *b*). Usually the free style is reserved for narrative or illustrative scenes, like the entries into Valhalla on the Sockburn stones or the stag hunts of Middleton and Stonegrave. The cross Middleton A (Plate II*b*) in one sense is very much a local monument in that its wheel-head type is confined to Ryedale and its dragon has a counterpart on the neighbouring cross, but its hunt scene speaks of more far ranging links with the Heysham hogback on the Irish Sea coast and perhaps with the bases of several Irish high crosses. The crystallized form of the motif, the 'hart and hound', is common on funerary sculpture throughout northern England: Yorkshire examples are found at Kirkleavington, Forcett, and Ellerburn, and a recently discovered carving at Stonegrave depicts the hunting of the stag by a bowman. The symbolism of the scene has yet to be satisfactorily interpreted; it seems unlikely that a society which rarely cut an inscription on a tombstone would be familiar with patristic references to Christian symbolism, especially since there is little run-of-the-mill Christian iconography on the majority of Anglo-Scandinavian stones. Its popularity may be another manifestation of the secular tastes of the patrons but there may also be some heroic or pagan reference half lost to us. A more cautious interpretation would be to see the stag hunt as purely decorative, culled from Irish or even Scottish models.

The likelihood of their having some significance is indicated by their style of carving. This free style is used elsewhere in Yorkshire to illustrate recognizable stories like Sigurd's killing of Fafnir and Regin (Lang 1976). Such a story is heroic rather than pagan and the juxtaposition of it with a Crucifixion at Kirkby Hill shows them to be compatible (Plate III*b*). Since the carvings pre-date the literary parallels and the Scandinavian carvings of the Sigurd sequence, the Yorkshire stones are crucial for an understanding of Viking-age versions of the myth. Moreover they point to an iconographic link with the contemporary sculpture on the Isle of Man. Certainly Sigurd scenes are now too common to be seen merely as dynastic references.

Some Yorkshire pieces fall between free style treatment and formalized ornamental design, thus complicating the interpretation of the subjects of their carving. The destroyed hogback from York Minster (Lang 1976, 93, fig 9) displayed a demi-figure with outstretched arms that were entwined by snakes whose heads closed in under the armpits. With Sigurd in mind it might be too easy to pronounce the figure to be Gunnar in the snake pit and to find fairly convincing Scandinavian analogues. On the other hand it could be a Crucifixion, since the recently discovered cross-head from St Mary Castlegate, York (Hall 1975, 24) and a crucifix at Sinnington both carry knotted snakes below Christ's arms (Plate III*f*). The bound Christ at Kirkdale and its fellow on the Jelling stone point to a late 10th century fashion that may have led to the snakes binding the arms.

It is safer to see the serpents as decorative fillers, as they appear as abstract interlace on the Kirkleavington crucifix (Plate III*e*). This cross-head is one of the few Yorkshire pieces that betrays unmistakable Irish influence. The extended upper arm, even in its dressed state, towers above the wheel and Christ's halo is similar to the reduced versions on the Castledermot crosses in Kildare (Henry 1967, pls 65, 66, & 70). This connection is reinforced by the presence at Castledermot of Ireland's only hogback, the recumbent monument of Anglo-Scandinavian Yorkshire (Lang 1971).

In stressing the secular nature of the Yorkshire sculpture it is easy to lose sight of monuments that continue in the Anglian tradition of ecclesiastical patronage. The large cross at Stonegrave (Plate III*d*), more than one commentator has suggested, has a distinct 'Celtic' character (Collingwood 1907b, 401; Binns 1956, 20). Certainly it is unlike any other cross in Yorkshire in its proportions, but it is also unlike any Irish cross in this respect. Similarly its wheel-head differs from the local Ryedale type, though its fan arms are typically late Anglian and their slender connecting wheel has a close parallel at Gargrave in the West Riding. Only two decorative details, the key fret and one of the figures, have Irish parallels. Rather than propose an ethnic stylistic influence, it is more important to make the point that the *orans* figure and the priest with his book satchel denote an ecclesiastical role for the cross, unlike the neighbouring Middleton - Kirkby Moorside series. The Stonegrave cross is an indication of the prosperity and influence of the church in Yorkshire during the 10th century.

The most impressive example of ecclesiastical sculpture from this period is the cross-shaft in Leeds parish church (Plate II*c*). Its portraits of draped and haloed figures continue the line from Otley, Ilkley, and Collingham, all Anglian monuments close to Leeds, and its vinescroll shows how tenaciously Anglian taste held in the West Riding. There are manuscript sources for some of the drapery and hair-styles that can only have existed in ecclesiastical centres, and its complex iconographic scheme of winged motifs drawn from Christian and heroic symbolism reveals an informed and subtle mind. Its Scandinavian feature is a spectacular one: the smith Volundr rising in his wings, a Norse hero among the cherubim and eagle of St John (Lang 1976, 90-2).

There may be an echo of the Leeds tradition elsewhere in Yorkshire at Bedale and at Sherburn, East Riding, and a shaft at Brompton depicts a cleric holding his maniple and wearing wings apparently strapped on like Volundr's. This Brompton shaft (Plate I*d*) has often been given too early a date because of its clerics' portraits and its vinescroll, but it undoubtedly belongs to the Allertonshire workshop that produced shafts for Kirkleavington and Sockburn (Plate I*e*). Its trademark is a ring placed on the top corner of the arris and the school is distinguished by adventurous, often nicely modelled figure carving. A shaft at Sockburn carries a profile portrait of a spearman wearing a ridged helmet and with a round shield (Knowles 1905, 115) and

Plate IVa   York Minster (photo: Alan Wiper)

Plate IVb   York Minster (photo: Alan Wiper)

Plate IVc   York Minster (photo: Alan Wiper)

Plate IVd   York Minster (photo: Alan Wiper)

Plate IVe   Brompton (photo: M Firby)

Plate IVf   Levisham (photo: J T Lang)

an identical secular warrior appears immediately below the vinescroll of the Brompton shaft, adjacent to the clerics. The vinescroll of this monument is a late form that develops even further on shafts like Middleton C and one from St Mary Bishophill Junior in York. It is barely naturalistic but reflects Anglian vinescroll growths and demonstrates the continuity of the old motifs alongside new fashions.

Perhaps the most surprising vinescroll of Anglo-Scandinavian Yorkshire is that on the Sutton on Derwent fragment (Plate IId). We have already seen how its sculptor copied the Folkton beasts; he also copied birds from York Minster and a Virgin from Nunburnholme. His vinescroll shows him to have been well travelled if eclectic, since the source of the pellet-filled, nicked leaf lies in the West Country: the door jambs at Britford, Wiltshire offer very close analogues, suggesting that Yorkshire was not totally isolated from southern English art (Kendrick 1938, pl LXXVI).

Yorkshire sculptors could, however, be innovative. Their most striking contribution was the recumbent monument, the hogback. The most spectacular examples are at Brompton and the distribution of the type seems to spread from Allertonshire, extending as far as the Cumbrian coast and generally being confined to those areas which are thought to have had a strong Norse-Irish presence. This coast to coast distribution conflicts with the precept that the Pennines formed a cultural barrier between 'Norse' to the west and 'Danes' to the east; stylistically there are many connections between Yorkshire and Cumbrian hogbacks.

The Brompton hogbacks represent a departure into three-dimensional sculpture (Plate IVe). The monument is a skeuomorph of a recognizable long-house with a curved, tegulated roof, its gables grasped by large muzzled bears. The naturalism is as innovative, compared with other Yorkshire animal ornament, as the three-dimensional treatment is alongside the customary low relief carving. The experiment was a minor one, however, as the most naturalistic of the Brompton bears are confined to only three hogbacks out of a total eleven from the site, and other examples from Brompton and neighbouring villages show a steady reversion to dragonesque or ornamental forms. Indeed, the end-beasts degenerate in the typological progression until they appear as grotesque masks like those at Barmston, East Riding and at sites in Ryedale.

The York Minster cemetery has provided the key to the immediate origin of the end-beasts of hogbacks, though they must be seen against a background of inward facing terminal heads, both in stone and in metal, stretching from Ireland to Scandinavia. The flat grave-slabs found under the Minster were laid over the length of the grave, and at each end rose a small headstone and footstone. There is some evidence at Penrith and at Inchcolm for hogbacks being used in conjunction with crosses to form such a composite monument. Now it is clear from the design of the York slabs that some of their animal ornament derives from late Anglian beasts like those at Ilkley, winged bipeds with interlace tails, so that an early 10th century date would be appropriate for their creation (Pattison 1973, pl 48 b-h). These animals occupy long panels flanking a central ridge which has diminutive animal-head terminals facing inwards. The winged beasts' heads fit the end of the panel so that, first, they are placed near the end of the grave and, secondly, they confront each other across the ridge immediately by the beast-head terminal of the ridge (Plate IVd). The Minster cemetery, however, is probably an 11th century one and it is clear that some of the slabs have been reused for the graves that Mr Phillips found them covering. Some of these slabs have been carefully cut

across so that the end piece could be used either to extend the length of the grave, as in Burial 9 (Pattison 1973, pls 39d and 48h), or to serve as a small headstone (Plate IVc). The Clifford Street piece is such a stone along with at least three others from the Minster (Pattison 1973, pls 48d and g, pls 49a and d). The resulting effect closely resembles the decorative lay-out of both the Fishergate ring (Cramp 1967, pl vii, b) and the headstone of Burial 2 (Pattison 1973, pl 52e and f), where a small head is squeezed between two confronting maned beasts (Plate IVa). This headstone is surely the result of copying the severed slab fragments already serving as uprights at a secondary stage. The Burial 2 headstone and footstone must therefore post-date the slabs. The headstone also has the appearance of a compressed hogback and it now seems probable that the large Allertonshire end-beasts are amplifications of the York predilection for confronted demi-beasts placed at the ends of graves.

The matching footstone from Burial 2 (Plate IVb) has outward facing heads but its most interesting, and tantalizing, feature is the pair of diagonal slots on each face (Pattison 1973, pl 52g and h). It is possible that these were intended as grooves for the timber planks of a coped composite monument of stone and wood.

The range and inventiveness of Anglo-Scandinavian sculpture in Yorkshire, its stylistic development within a relatively confined area, and its dependence on local sources, so often Anglian ones, all underline the distinctiveness of this flourishing art form. It is unjust to the sculptors to see the carvings as insular reflections of mainstream Scandinavian art and the closer the scrutiny of the stones, the less applicable become the Viking art style labels of Borre, Mammen, and Jellinge.

Gauber high pasture, Ribblehead— an interim report

A King

Introduction

While surveying the considerable areas of Romano-British field systems and associated settlements which are to be found on all flanks of the Ingleborough massif, W H Walker and the writer chanced upon a large stone-based structure, its adjoining outbuildings, and fields, in 1964 (King & Walker 1966). The prehistoric and Romano-British settlement patterns in the valleys and on the terraces and plateaux of the Carboniferous limestone at altitudes of 180m-360m, away from centres of later ploughing, have been and are being published elsewhere (King, A, 1969; 1970). The large stone-based building of this Gauber High Pasture site at Ribblehead (henceforward Ribblehead) appeared incongruous when compared with the smaller rectangular and circular stone-based dwellings of the 2nd-4th centuries AD. Not being the major facet of the research, the site was spared all but the attention of rockery stone collectors until 1974, when the nearby limestone quarry changed ownership. It was clear from the construction of new railway sidings that Amey Roadstone, the new owners, would work the limestone, and, in advance of quarrying, would remove the weathered limestone pavements, for which planning consent to quarry had been given previously.

The site under discussion was inside the area of planning consent, so, with funding from the Carnegie Trust UK, a training excavation was mounted. Subsequently, in the summers of 1975 and 1976, the excavation became a rescue project financed by the Department of the Environment, with the support of North Yorkshire County Council (Education Dept) through Ingleborough Centre, Ingleton.

The Ribblehead site lies at an altitude of 340m OD. This level is the topmost bed of the white Great Scar limestone, on the northern flank of Park Fell, which itself comprises alternating dark limestones, sandstones, and shales to a height of 564m. One kilometre to the east is the River Ribble flowing south, while two kilometres to the west, Winterscales Beck runs south-westward into the Lune. The Lancaster-Bainbridge (Wensleydale) Roman road utilizes the pass emphasizing the trans-Pennine significance of the site (Fig 4).

Work commenced in 1974 with the aim of excavating all but the wall foundations; these, it was hoped, would be preserved for as long as possible. The northern quarter of Building A (54m²) and all of Building C (72m²) were stripped. Consequent upon the findings of the initial season's work, the Department of the Environment funded the 1975 work, when the southern half of Building A (90m²) was excavated. The remainder of that building, the adjacent one to the north, Building B, and an investigation of the associated enclosed land, was undertaken with further DoE monies in 1976.

The buildings and enclosures

The three buildings on the site all have paved entrances from a farmyard, which in turn had three apparent openings in the enclosure wall on its eastern, western, and northern sides. To the north-east of the farmyard are two slightly larger plots enclosed with limestone walls. To the south, on a drift-covered surface between two limestone terraces, are two fields with a combined area of almost an acre and a half (0.51 ha).

Building A is the largest of the three buildings, measuring 19.52m or 18.91m by 3.96m internally (Fig 5). The floor is reasonably rectangular, though the internal faces of the nothern wall are out of alignment by 0.6m. The long walls are 1.5-1.8m thick, though at one point they thin to 1.43m. The inner face is of coursed limestone slabs, the outer is less well defined, being a boulder kerb of single stones. The wall fill is limestone rubble. The gable ends, though typologically similar, with centrally placed paved doorways, contrast in strength. The southern example is massively built with individual stones weighing over 50 kilos, and measures 2.84m and 3.04m thick, at the junctions with the internal faces of the long walls (Plate V). The northern end wall is less solid with some domestic refuse and other finds occurring in the earth and rubble fill; it measures approximately 2.44m thick. The end walls are curved, the outer edge of each long wall describing an almost perfect semi-circle terminating at the door jamb (Plate VI). The narrow 0.61m wide southern doorway complements the massive masonry, while, at the opposite end, the doorway measures 0.91m. The floor slopes downward to the north, and there is a difference of 1.02m between the levels of the two doorway pavings.

In places, the limestone bed rock projected through the turf in the building's interior before excavation. These outcropping clints and their associated solution gullies made interpretation of internal features difficult. It was not possible to identify a posthole or hearth, although along the western wall in the northern part of the building, a low kerb of limestones running parallel to and against sandstone paving is interpreted as the edge of a 4.28m long bench. Architecturally, it is perhaps worth mentioning that three 'shoes' were found along the inner face of the west wall. Each shoe comprises the wall face and two slabs built out of the wall ar right-angles to it. Two of these three compartments contained a hemispherical gritstone, the dressed flat fracture surface uppermost.

Building C differs from the other buildings (Plate VII). It is a poorly built sub-rectangular structure, 9m × 5m. The two long walls are both built directly on to two bedrock limestone surfaces, the facing edges of which are about 3m apart. It is not possible to say whether the limestone had been denuded of its soil and vegetation cover naturally, or whether the builders stripped off what must have been a thin veneer.

The two end walls are built up from the bottom of the gully or space between the two outcrops. The western side is naturally higher than its opposite number, the bottom course level being 0.7m above floor level, compared with 0.5m. The paved doorway is in the southern end of the eastern long wall with an external limestone doorstep; the

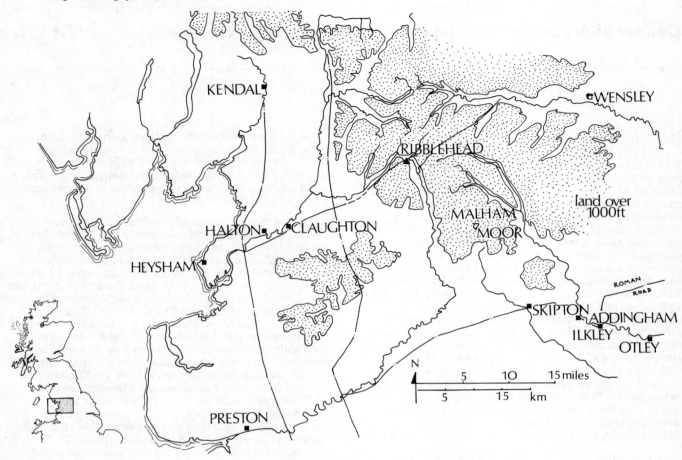

Fig 4   Gauber High Pasture, Ribblehead—site location map

paving is limited to a zone along the southern part of the floor not more than 1m wide. The remainder of the floor is clay, with a considerable amount of shattered sandstone pieces bedded or trodden in near the doorway. A broken sandstone hearth was found placed virtually in the centre of the unpaved floor.

Building B is also sub-rectangular and measures internally 6m × 3.3-3.7m (Plate VII). The walls are solidly built in limestone, averaging 1.7-1.9m thick. The doorway is positioned at the western end of the southern long wall and is entered via a double walled, sandstone paved approach or passage at least 4m long. This feature widens from 0.65m at the door to about 1.05m. The sandstone paving continues into the building where it is found predominantly in the western half. The floor level rises to the other end, where two blocks of bedrock remain 0.5m above floor level. Behind these blocks, in the arc of the north-eastern corner, is a feature exhibiting a narrow 0.2m flue with at the bottom a layer of broken sandstones covered by a layer of limestone slabs. This feature is interpreted as an oven or kiln.

A boulder wall continues the line of the interior facing of the northern wall to the east. There is no trace of another edge to that wall, nor of any wall fill; it may be a badly robbed wall but this is considered unlikely.

Finds

At the time of writing, a number of finds are being treated in conservation laboratories and some await further analysis. However, sufficient meaningful identification has been

made to justify drawing attention to the discoveries.

A suite of iron objects was found on the paving outside the northern doorway of the large building. Immediately recognizable were two angle backed knife blades, 100mm and 80mm long respectively, and one half of a bipartite horse bit measuring 75mm. It is assumed this broke on the loop linking the two halves. What was considered in the field to be a sword—a quantity of wood was adhering to the iron at the end of the blade—turned out to be a socketed spearhead when reconstructed in the British Museum laboratory. The blade is 0.41m long with a maximum width of 25mm, but the socket is obviously incomplete, adding only 100mm to the length of the blade. Miscellaneous metal fragments were discovered in Building B and one small wrought iron clapper bell, which measures a mere 50mm overall, might be described as a cow bell.

The only other metal objects so far identified are four Northumbrian *stycas*. The first, found in 1974, belongs to the reign of Aethelred II and is by the moneyer Odilo. The second, found in 1975, was struck for Archbishop Wulfhere by the moneyer Wulfred. The other *stycas* are both blundered but one is most likely to have been minted within five years of the last mentioned coin.

The more important lithic finds are a small lathe-turned green stone spindle whorl and two slipper-shaped stones smoothed on their wider surfaces but exhibiting the marks of hammering along their sides, all found in Building C. The matching top and bottom stones of a rotary quern were discovered in Building B.

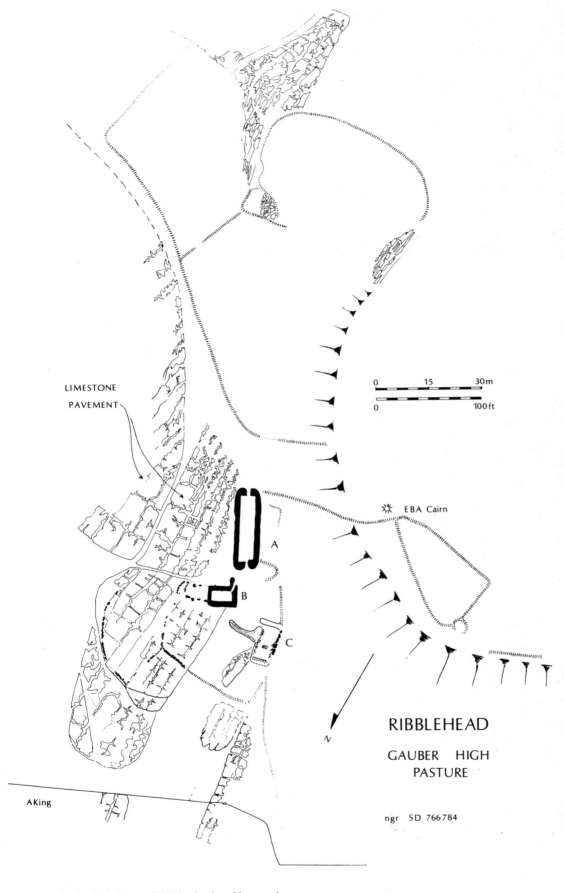

LIMESTONE
PAVEMENT

EBA Cairn

A

B

C

RIBBLEHEAD

GAUBER HIGH
PASTURE

ngr SD 766784

AKing

Fig 5   Gauber High Pasture, Ribblehead—plan of farmstead

Plate V   Ribblehead building A: the centrally placed doorway in the southern gable (photo: A King)

Plate VI   Ribblehead: the largest of the farmstead buildings photographed from the north. The curving gable swinging outward from the inner pair of metric ranging poles positioned in the doorway. Limestone pavement outside the doorway (photo: A King)

Plate VII   Ribblehead building C: this workshop has a sandstone slab hearth in an approximately central position (photo: A King)

Discussion

The three rectangular buildings open into one enclosure, with Buildings A and B sharing a common expanse of paving between their two adjacent doorways. There can be little doubt that the double walled exit from Building B was meant to shelter people moving regularly into Building A, though there is no evidence to suggest the passageway was roofed. The smaller, more earthfast Building C is a poor architectural specimen. The central hearth suggests an opening in the roof to let out the smoke, and the discovery of iron rich cinders and sharpening-cum-hammerstones imply this was a workshop, possibly a smithy. Maybe the warmth of the hearth attracted someone to spin in that structure, though there is always the likelihood that the spindle whorl had been turned on a lathe in that workshop and had never produced thread. The stone is the same as that used in the hammerstones, an Ingletonian greywacke, found not closer than two miles away from the site.

Building B too yielded evidence suggesting that some craft processes were carried out inside but the strongest indications, a concentration of small animal bones, the quern, and the oven or kiln are all connected with food preparation, making this the kitchen building. The position of the almost circular oven or kiln in the north-east corner makes the building of a chimney or flue possible. It is likely that the lower horizon of sandstone flags was the floor of the oven and that the limestone slabs comprised its roof. A report by James Rackham on the animal bones will appear elsewhere but they were kindly identified for me earlier by Colin Sims. It is perhaps sufficient to say here that most of the bones were from cattle, sheep or goat, and horse. Red deer and pig, possibly wild boar, are present in much smaller quantities, with a small number of game birds, hare and, surprisingly, the jaw of a fox. Mr Sims has shown that many of the animals were adult and were butchered.

Interpreting the date of Buildings B and C and their physical form is reasonably simple, but this is not so for Building A. It was mentioned above that the floor dropped 1.02m from the southern doorway to the northern one and that no postholes could be identified with any certainty: however, the way the paving swings from along the centre axis to the western side in the middle of the building attests a partition. The same sandstone paving in the northern half lies against and emphasizes a row of small limestones, which must be the kerb of a wallbench. It was from the hypothetical rear edge of this bench and the wall face that the only animal bones resulting from meat eating in this building were found. The occupants were alas otherwise remarkably fastidious.

Plate V shows Building A from the north, with the internal edge of the north end wall marked by the 2m ranging poles. From the central pair, positioned as doorposts, the external wall faces—excavated but for the basal horizon—can be seen curving around to become the outer edges of the long walls. Between the arcs of the kerbs are the fine quality and very unusual limestone paving slabs. It was on this surface that the two broken knife blades and the spearhead were discovered. The interior face of the western portion of the end wall is incomplete, unless access was needed to the wall core, where two of the coins were found. One other coin was found lying on an end wall kerb stone and one on the paving immediately outside. The position and dating of the coins is most important. They all belong to the third quarter of the 9th century, and may date the building of this farmhouse or may pre-date

it; but as they lie low down in the wall they cannot post-date the building.

In discussions on site, it has been suggested that this close scatter of *stycas* was a disturbed hoard, dispersed by the builders in their excavation work. The writer does not agree with this view, considering it more likely that the three in the wall, within 1.2m of one another, were close to their original position, while the one on the outside paving, physically 0.3m lower, had been moved naturally to its find spot. It must be emphasized that the finds belong to one contemporary assemblage.

The final inquiries must attempt to resolve some of the architectural detail of this large farmhouse. It cannot be called a longhouse, as there is no positive evidence that cattle were ever housed inside, though some may take the not very convincing negative view that as there is no evidence of cattle having been housed in a shippon, or in the workshop, they must have been housed in the largest building. Clearly all the buildings had ridged roofs with a thatch or eventually a turf roof extending to a point close to the external edge of the wall. It is inconceivable with these almost drystone limestone walls that the roof should have shed its rain anywhere else. The form of the roof at the ends of the building remains a point to be resolved. Was there a straight gable end with semi-circular walls projecting beyond? It seems more likely that some form of hipped roof or porch was held up by timbers springing from the kerb.

Conclusion

The interpretation of Ribblehead, its buildings, its architecture, and the relevance of the excavated finds, will change, as a number of analyses are completed and published. Views may also crystallize as a result of this paper and the ensuing debate; the writer believes that the site will be spared for at least five years and that visitors will be allowed to view it.

The farmstead probably traded with Lunesdale and Morecambe Bay, not with Wensleydale or York. The problem is to isolate materials that were obviously imported a distance. Scrutiny eliminates all but the iron objects, and there is more than a suggestion that some of those could have been manufactured on site.

At the moment the site still poses one major question—is the farmstead *landnam* Norse Viking or typically Northumbrian Anglo-Saxon or was there continuity in this locality from the time of the breakdown of Roman military influence? At present it would be unreasonable to answer the question. It is sufficient to write that the excavation was a rare breakthrough focusing the minds of archaeologists and historians on marginal land use in the north-west.

Acknowledgements

I would like to thank all those who worked at Ribblehead during the three seasons of excavation and those people who made the excavation possible. I refer to members of Carnegie UK Trust and to the Department of the Environment, Ancient Monuments Section, for providing financial support. Particular mention must be made of Mr P Metcalfe, tenant, and the directors, management, and workmen of Amey Roadstone Corporation for permission to excavate and the many kindnesses which made the work easier. Finally may I thank my academic friends who visited the site, set off hares, and generally helped answer some of the questions.

The Anglo-Danish and Anglo-Norse coinages of York

Michael Dolley

At the beginning of the last third of the 9th century the pagan Danes destroyed the Christian kingdom of Northumbria. They themselves were coinless, and they terminated a coinage of copper totally anomalous where the rest of Western Europe was concerned. For a generation the new Anglo-Danish society appears to have made do without coins, though trade contacts with Europe rather than the rest of England may have introduced a proportion of sub-Carolingian silver *deniers*. Just before the year 900 everything changed. Put out by the largely Christianized Danes of York was a very substantial coinage of silver pence with a few halfpence. Not uncharacteristic is a coin with on one side a cross and the legend MIRABILIA FECIT ('He has done wonderful things') and on the other a small cross flanked by two pellets dividing a contracted legend to be expanded Dom*iNu*S D*eu*S/*Omnipotens* REX ('The Lord God Almighty King'). Such pieces mule into an extensive series where on one side the enigmatic legend CUNNETTI surrounds a cross, while on the other the letters C-N-U-T and R-E-X are disposed around a symbol usually described as a patriarchal cross (Fig 6). The obvious

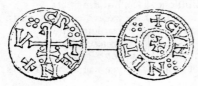

Fig 6

interpretation is 'King Cnut', and there seems much to be said for Dr A P Smyth's suggestion that we identify him with the Danish incomer Knutr who *c* 900 fought battles north of Cleveland and near Scarborough, and who was killed at Dublin in 903 (?). Certainly an Irish nexus accords well with the circumstance that all but a handful of his extant coins derive from the great Cuerdale treasure recovered from the banks of the Ribble above Preston in 1840. Mr James Graham-Campbell rightly insists on the 'Irish' flavour of the hacksilver and ingots accompanying the coins, and the most plausible interpretation of the treasure is that it had been brought there by Norse refugees from Dublin when the Irish of Meath temporarily expelled the Scandinavian inhabitants. To judge from the site they appear to have been attempting to force a crossing rather than push up the valley, but their ultimate objective must have been York, home for the Danish survivors of Knutr's abortive intervention in Ireland and a possible place of refuge for their Norse cousins and quondam allies.

The CNUT REX coins in turn are linked with an only slightly less extensive and apparently slightly earlier coinage in the name of a SIEFREDUS REX (Fig 7), and

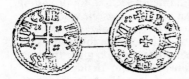

Fig 7

this could well be the Sigfrid or Sigeferth who appears to have succeeded Guthfrith as king of the Danes of York *c* 895 after descents on Wessex and Dublin. Probably later than the CNUT REX coins, on the other hand, are some very rare pieces with the name ALWALDU*s* (Fig 8), and it has been suggested, not very convincingly, that they

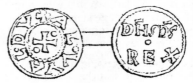

Fig 8

reflect a brief acceptance by the Danes of York of a nephew of Ælfred the Great, Æthelwald by name, who took refuge with the Vikings after an unsuccessful attempt to dispute the succession of his cousin Edward the Elder in 899. What is indisputable, however, is that the SIEFREDUS REX and CNUT REX coins and their regally anonymous analogues constitute the first coins of the York Vikings, and that the earliest of them were not struck for at least two decades after the 876 plantation of Yorkshire by all but the most militant of that wing of the Great Army which had followed Halfdan into Northumbria the previous year. Exceptionally rare coins which essay the name Halfdan are now recognized as belonging to the Danish Midlands and to the 890s, and have nothing at all to do with the Halfdan killed on Strangford Lough in 877.

What can scarcely be stressed overmuch is that this, the first Viking coinage of York, looks not to England but to the Continent. Indeed an earlier generation of numismatists was inclined to read into the reverse legend EBRAICE CIV*itas* found on some of the coins the mint-signature not of York but of Evreux (Fig 9), and certainly there are close

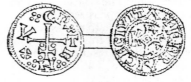

Fig 9

affinities between the York coins and certain Viking pieces struck at Quentovic near the modern Calais. It is a coinage of sea-kings that concerns us, and sea-kings of the North Sea, for all their occasional forays into the waters off Ireland and western Scotland.

The Cuerdale treasure is believed to have been lost in 903, and the septennium that follows is one of the most obscure in the whole of the history of Northumbria. What is known, however, is that there began *c* 905 a new coinage of York with an overtly ecclesiastical flavour. On the one side the EBRAICE CIV*itas* legend soon gives way to the more familiar and unambiguous EBORACE CIV*itas* ('City of York'), though the type of the cross is retained, while on the other there appears a two-line legend S*an*C*t*I PETRI

MO*neta* ('St Peter's money'). Symptomatic of a new political orientation is the circumstance that relatively few of these coins seem to have found their way to Scandinavia or to the Continent, whereas in finds from the Irish Sea littoral they are relatively common. The idiom still is not English though perhaps less obtrusively so, but after no more than a few years there is a marked deterioration in the weight and the quality of execution if not in the purity of the alloy. It is hard not to see in this the reflection of some catastrophe, and we do well to remember that in 910 York attempted to halt the advance of Wessex and Mercia at the expense of the Danes settled in the Trent valley and East Anglia. At the battle of Tettenhall near Wolverhampton the Danish leadership was decimated, and Dr Smyth rightly stresses the importance of this bloodbath in shaping the fortunes of York over the next generation and more. In modern jargon the Danes of Northumbria experienced a leadership vacuum, and the numismatic evidence supports most but not quite all of Dr Smyth's interpretation of the advent on the York scene of a certain Ragnall from Dublin.

This Ragnall is termed in the Irish sources a grandson of Ívarr, and Dr Smyth is not the first to have identified this Ívarr who ruled Dublin around 860 with the celebrated Ívarr nicknamed 'the Boneless' who toppled the English kingdoms of Northumbria and East Anglia in the ensuing decade. Two late sources (not just one) agree, however, that Ívarr the Boneless was childless, and so by definition could not have had grandsons, and there is no need to suppose a Danish ancestry to explain Ragnall's attraction for the Danes of York. Just as in 1912 Ulster rallied behind a Dublin lawyer and sixty years later conceded a quite remarkable personal ascendancy to a Welsh professor of Greek, so York in the aftermath of the débâcle at Tettenhall was perfectly prepared to settle for alien leadership provided only that it was positive and promised to be effective. Around 914, then, we find Ragnall campaigning in what is now Northumberland, and establishing a toe-hold in England before going off to join his brothers and cousins in an Irish venture which in three brief years restored Waterford, Limerick, and Dublin to Norse control. It cannot well be coincidence that *c* 915 is the most natural slot for some

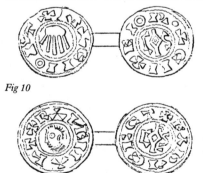

Fig 10

Fig 11

rare York coins with an obverse legend RAIENALT and such novel types as a Thor's hammer, a bow-and-arrow, a form of the Karolus monogram (Figs 10 and 11), and a profile bust, the last two derived respectively from Continental and English models.

We are not to imagine that the 'doves' among the Danes of York welcomed with open arms the militantly pagan Ragnall, and disorder promised ill for trade, a matter of some concern in a worsening economic climate. It is not surprising, then, that many of the Danes of York wondered whether more might not be gained from English

overlordship, and the death of the widowed Æthelflæd of Mercia in 917 appears to have cut short a phase of delicate negotiation which might have advanced her brother Edward the Elder's northern frontier to the Tyne instead of the Trent. As it was, in 919 Ragnall returned to Northumbria and was accepted as king at York. He died only two years later, but we may perhaps associate with this interlude some rare coins struck to a somewhat higher standard which have as their types a simple form of Thor's hammer and a Viking sword. The legends are meaningless, but the idiom is that of the coinage that follows rather than that of what has gone before.

Ragnall's successor was another of the grandsons of Ívarr of Dublin, a brother or half-brother possibly but perhaps a cousin. This was a certain Sihtric or Sigtryggr variously nicknamed 'Caoch' or 'Caech' with reference to a defect in one or both of his eyes or else 'Gale' in respect of his ethnic origin. Of this undoubted king of York —in 925 he married a half-sister of the English king Æthelstan—not a dozen coins are known. The obverse type is a sword that divides a two-line legend SITRIC REX ('King Sihtric'), though in one case the title is the unexplained

Fig 12

LUDO instead of REX. The reverses fall into two groups, one with cross (Fig 12) and one with either of two forms of the Thor's hammer, and there is the possibility that some may have been struck at a mint other than York. Lincoln comes to mind, and there are from this critical quinquennium some very rare coins with the same types but with the sword dividing a legend S*an*C*t*I MARTI*ni* ('St Martin's')

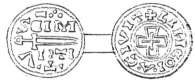

Fig 13

and an unequivocal Lincoln mint-signature (Fig 13). More and more, numismatists are recognizing that it was Æthelstan and not Edward the Elder who advanced the English frontier from the Trent to the Humber, and it is interesting that Sihtric's coins are accompanied by slightly more common pennies in the name of St Peter but with the sword added to the obverse type. These again have

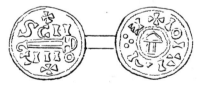

Fig 14

two types of reverse, a cross with an unintelligible legend or one or other of two forms of Thor's hammer and an essay at the York mint-signature (Fig 14).

All these coins, Sihtric's as well as those with the names of the two saints, are of superior execution and weight to those that have gone before, and the injection of new blood and (?) capital seems obvious. More than a century ago that greatly underrated English numismatist Daniel Haigh suggested that the sword of the obverse type was that of Carlus, one of the prized cult-objects of the Norse of Dublin, and the mingling of Christian and pagan symbols argues for a certain recrudescence of heathenism. This all accords well with the historical intrusion of the Dubliners under Ragnall and Sihtric into the affairs of north-eastern England between 919 and 927, while an essential coexistence of the two religions is neatly pointed by the occurrence on some coins of a small version of Thor's hammer actually below the name of the prince of the apostles. Christianity could afford to be tolerant, and the 'good luck' symbol involved was perhaps no more offensive than the horse-shoe on a modern wedding-cake. Although, too, the types of this York coinage of the early 920s are still distinctive, the fabric is becoming more 'English', and we have come a certain way from the position which obtained a quarter of a century earlier when the issues of the York mint not only imitated those of the Continent but stood out from other insular series like the proverbial 'sore thumb'.

Equally changed is the whole pattern of discovery. Whereas the issues of *c* 900 are known almost exclusively from one massive hoard, that from Cuerdale, those of *c* 905–*c* 920 are from a range of smaller finds from York itself, Yorkshire, Cumberland, Lancashire, Cheshire, Norfolk, and central and eastern Ireland. This is not to say that the odd piece has not occurred to the east of the North Sea, but we are reminded that an important factor in the English resurgence under Edward the Elder and his sister Æthelflæd was a loosening of ties between the Danes settled in England and their kinsmen in Denmark. A generation before this a comparable severance of the umbilical cord with Norway had left the Norse of the Scottish Isles and of Ireland to 'go it alone', and mutual shortages of manpower doubtless explain the increasing interdependence of York and Dublin in the first half of the 10th century. The relatively small number of York coins from the early 920s have find-spots not just in Yorkshire, Lincolnshire, and Norfolk, but also in North Wales, Scotland, and above all Ireland. A hint at the nascent power of a Lowlands-based Scottish monarchy is afforded by the failure of the numismatic evidence to lend support to the too ingenious hypothesis that there was extensive use of the Clyde-Forth isthmus. All the evidence of the coins is that in their comings and goings the Vikings of York and their Dublin cousins traversed the Pennine passes. The Cuerdale hoard in fact sets a pattern culminating appropriately enough in the 954 slaying of the fugitive Eric Bloodaxe at Stainmore.

Sihtric died only a few months after concluding a marriage alliance with the English king's half-sister, and his son Anlaf (ON O*lafr*) appears to have been considered too young to succeed him. The leadership of the Hiberno-Norse of York passed to yet another of Ívarr's grandsons, a certain Guthfrith, and cause for further confusion in the already tangled historical record is the circumstance that his son also bore the name Anlaf. No coins with Guthfrith's name are known, and it must remain a moot point whether perhaps abandonment of coinage in his own name was part of the price paid by Sihtric for his English marriage. On the other hand, Guthfrith's rule at York was ephemeral in the extreme, and by July 927 Æthelstan had occupied the city and was interfering decisively in the affairs of Northumbria. It was not long, too, before Guthfrith and both the Anlafs were in Ireland giving new impetus to Dublin's ill-judged assault upon Munster which by showing up the incapacity of the Eoghenacht dynasty of

Cashel would in the long run bring to power a High King able at once to defeat and to use the Norse of Ireland. York remained a magnet, however, and especially for Guthfrith and his son. While Æthelstan lived English arms guaranteed their exclusion, and from 927 until 939 the York mint struck coins in the English king's name and on the English model. Even so, an underlying separateness is still discernible and best seen, perhaps, in the replacement over much of the period of the normal college of moneyers by a single individual.

In 937 Anlaf Guthfrithsson invaded northern England only to receive a bloody nose at the great battle of Brunanburh, but there is no obvious interruption of coinage at York to suggest that Æthelstan's hold on Northumbria was seriously challenged. It was very different in 939 when Æthelstan had not been dead for more than a very few weeks before Anlaf Guthfrithsson seized York, and in the following year made himself master of the English Midlands from the Trent to the Wash. Within months coins with his name were being struck not just at York but also at Derby, and the earliest at the latter mint even employed reverse dies that appear to have been intended for use with Æthelstan obverses. At York the most spectacular coins, though far from rare, are those with a raven as the obverse type and the royal style CUNUNC (ON *Konungr*) (Fig 15). The fabric, however, is purely

Fig 15

English, and the reverse indistinguishable except by its legend from a common obverse and reverse of Æthelstan. Such pieces had little trouble in circulating beside English coins, and the odd specimen has occurred in a whole range of finds from Scotland and Ireland. A curious detail is that there is only one moneyer, and it would seem that the Hiberno-Norse king had taken over lock, stock, and barrel the minting arrangements of his predecessor.

In 941 Anlaf Guthfrithsson switched his theatre of operations to the territories north of the Tees which a quarter of a century earlier had first attracted his kinsman (uncle?) Ragnall. Again he was victorious, but within a matter of weeks he died, and most of his conquests were lost by his inadequate successors. First to arrive on the scene was his cousin Anlaf Sihtricsson nicknamed Cuaran ('of the sandal') who was unable to prevent Eadmund of England bringing the frontier back to the Humber by dint of a campaign which English propaganda was able to represent as a liberation where the Danish population of the East Midlands was concerned. To judge from the coins he was joined by a certain Sihtric, a brother perhaps, who may be the 'Sihtric of the Jewels' whom later tradition associated with a humiliation of Dublin at the hands of Muirchertach ('Moriarty') nicknamed 'of the leather cloaks', and quite possibly the Sihtric killed a year or two later during one of the last Viking descents upon France. It was doubtless their failure to hold onto the conquests of 940 that prompted the intervention of the dead Anlaf's brother, another Ragnall who is better known to the numismatist as Regnald from the spelling of his name invariably employed upon the coins. Of Sihtric just two coins have survived. One, found in Rome, is of purely English type, and but for the legends would pass as English. The other, probably found in Ireland, is of very English fabric but has for its obverse type a trilobed ornament usually described as a triquetra, and on the reverse a triangular Viking standard topped by a small cross. The symbolism was not inappropriate. The archbishop of York had ridden south with Anlaf Guthfrithsson in 940 and actually negotiated the revision of the English frontier, and during the next few months Christianity was courted alike by Anlaf Sihtricsson and by Regnald Guthfrithsson in a vain attempt to avert an English reconquest of Northumbria. Only less rare than the Sihtric penny are pieces with the same types and the names of the cousins Anlaf and Regnald (Fig 16), and these continue the style CUNUNC instead of REX. To the literate it would have been clear that the

Fig 16

coins were struck by an authority other than English, and it was perhaps because the criterion was so immediately obvious that the alien style was abandoned. With the next issue there was still no reversion to REX, after which two generations would elapse before CUNUNC was ephemerally revived on rare coins of Dublin by Sihtric nicknamed 'Silkbeard', a grandson (?) of Anlaf and great-nephew (?) of Regnald.

To the numismatist the York coins of 943 and 944 exhibit remarkable diversity, but superficially they correspond too closely to English prototypes to be exciting to a non-specialist. Shared by Anlaf and Regnald is a modification of a common type of Æthelstan where the cross pattée of the obverse is replaced by a cross moline

Fig 17

(Fig 17). Corroboration of their York origin comes from a lead trial-piece (or mint-weight?) now in the British Museum but apparently found in York which bears the imprint of two reverse dies with the names of different moneyers. Struck for Anlaf by York moneyers are even rarer pennies with a reverse type of a flower modelled on coins of Derby—indeed it is only recently that Mr C E Blunt has argued that they are not Derby coins of the cousin. They are followed by relatively common coins again reading REX which imitate the standard English penny of the period. The obverse type is a small cross pattée, while the reverse has the name of the moneyer in two lines with

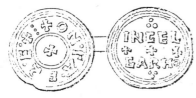

Fig 18

crosses between and a trefoil above and below (Fig 18). On the earlier pieces the king's name is still spelt ANLAF but on the later it is ONLAF or OLOF.

By the end of 944 Regnald was dead, and Anlaf back in Dublin. Both had accepted baptism in an attempt to enlist English support, but the gesture cut no ice with Eadmund the political realist, and the reincorporation of Northumbria into England was achieved with relative ease. Interestingly there appears to have been no victimization of the men who had struck coins for the Hiberno-Norse interlopers. Almost without exception they are found over the next few years striking for Eadmund and for his successor Eadred. It is a reminder of early medieval tolerance in a happier age before decadent feudalism became obsessed with treason. This is not to say that there was not an element of self-interest if not expediency in royal generosity. Until 867 Northumbria had been an independent Anglian kingdom with aspirations to English hegemony, and one did not have to be of Scandinavian descent to resent the pretensions of the West Saxon royal house risen to greatness on the ruins of an older order overthrown by Viking invasion. The archbishop of York himself would have to be brought south to cool his heels under house-arrest, and the strength of persisting separatist sentiment was made very obvious in the autumn of 947 when Northumbria accepted as king the exiled Eric of Norway with the suggestive nickname 'Bloodaxe'. English alarm was understandable even if the chances of a putsch back in Norway reviving a grand design on the Anglo-Celtic Isles were in fact remote. For one thing modern scholarship has come to appreciate that the imperialism of Harald nicknamed 'Fairhair', Eric's father, was largely invented at the end of the 11th century to give respectability to the novel ambitions of Magnus nicknamed 'Barelegs'. For another there still did not exist a Norway with the capacity to mount a national enterprise on a scale proportionate to English fears. Eadred, however, was taking no chances, and in 948 an English army expelled Eric, but not before he had struck a number of coins of purely English type, the moneyers being those who had served the Hiberno-Norse kings and the English monarchy with equal attention to the commercial needs of the community. What does surprise is that in 949 Eadred appears to have acquiesced in the return to York of Anlaf Sihtricsson, for the Dubliners a fatal dissipation of resources urgently needed if the reduction of Munster was ever to be achieved. It could be that England felt that the overstretched Hiberno-Norse were the lesser of two evils and even some sort of guarantee against the dreaded Eric's return, but this is pure speculation. What is certain is that what must rank as one of the most apolitical mints of all times seems to have had no difficulty in adjusting to the new political situation. The same moneyers who had struck intermittently for Eadmund, Eadred and Eric now put out a coinage with the English type of Eric's but the legend ONLAF REX.

In 952 another change of fortune brought back Eric who appears this time to have appreciated the importance of cultivating the Hiberno-Norse element in York society. However this may be, what proved in the event to be the last coins struck for an autonomous York revived the type of a sword from a generation before. The obverse is that of Sihtric Caoch with the simple substitution of Eric's name, and the reverse the English type of a small cross that goes back by way of both Anlafs and Regnald to

Fig 19

Æthelstan (Fig 19). The moneyers remain the same, and in 954 when the English army finally expelled Eric they again made their peace with Eadred and continued to strike for his successors.

The pattern of finding of the York coins of the fifteen years 939-954 is once more suggestive. The odd specimen has come from as far afield as Scandinavia, Brittany, and Rome—but always in the company of the English pennies they so closely resembled—but the basic drift was westwards to the Irish Sea and so to Ireland. Even Eric's abortive career reveals that any effective political nexus with Scandinavia was nugatory, and it was to a similarly and also increasingly embattled Dublin that separatist sentiment looked for support. The emergence, partly as a response to the 9th century Viking assaults, of new national monarchies in England and Ireland, and to a lesser degree Scotland, was having political consequences affecting the Scandinavian settlements in the Anglo-Celtic Isles as a whole. For example, the Viking settlers on Man who until now had held aloof from the affairs of their neighbours identify with Dublin through a dynasty expelled from Limerick, and it is only with the 960s that we have coin-hoards from the island, which perhaps makes it the more remarkable that two of them should contain no fewer than six of the 939-954 coins of Viking kings of York, one of Anlaf Guthfrithsson, three of Anlaf Sihtricsson, and two of Eric Bloodaxe.

From 954 onwards York was an English mint. Its products conformed to a national norm, and the economic advantages of its recognition of political reality can be gauged from the fact that for more than a century it was the second most important mint in England, giving pride of place only to London and heading off with ease the competition of Lincoln and Winchester. If the coinage ceases to be distinct, on the other hand, it remains distinctive. Under Eadgar (957/959-975), for example, a *circumscription* variety without mint-signature was struck on a scale unmatched further to the south, and belated recognition of the fact that certain *three-line* pennies only appearing to bear the York mint-signature in fact hail from the other side of the Pennines means that the shape of the York coinage acquires a new clarity. Around the year 973 the local production of dies appears to have been interrupted as part of a move to centralization based on London, but by the end of the decade York was not only producing a majority of the dies required by its own mint but supplying a number to other mints in north-eastern England. Royal jealousy may even explain why *c* 985 the York mint, along with that of Lincoln, failed to participate in the second substantive coinage of Æthelræd II (978-1016). Striking resumed in or about the year 991, but it was not until after the millennium that dies once more were engraved locally. From then until well into the reign of Cnut the Great (1016-1035) York was not just a major mint but also a most important centre for the cutting of dies. Under Edward the Confessor (1042-1066) again there are at least two occasions, one in the late 1040s and the other just before the end of the reign, when a proportion of the dies appear to have been produced at York instead of London, and numismatists have still to come up with a convincing explanation of why in every type of the reign but the third the reverse dies of York coins should be marked with an annulet in the field. When in the early 1050s, too, there was a general move throughout England to reduce the number of moneyers striking in any given mint, York received notably preferential treatment by being allowed a college with as many as twelve. Nor does the northern metropolis appear to have been victimized on account of events in the autumn of 1065 when—shades of 940—the men of York advanced deep into the English Midlands and actually harried beyond Watling Street before being persuaded to return to their allegiance. From the Scandinavian coin-hoards, moreover, it is clear that York traded extensively across the North Sea. It was not an Anglo-Saxon but a Norman king who ended Anglo-Danish York's period of greatness, and the economic consequences of the harrying of the north are nowhere seen more clearly than in the city's coinage. Twelve moneyers still were striking when William the Conqueror (1066-1087) paid his first visit to his new territories north of the Humber, but soon there were only four. More is known, too, concerning the so-called *Paxs* coinage put out during the last years of his reign than about any other of the coinages of the years 1066-1154, and it is a commentary on the impoverishment of York at the end of the Anglo-Danish period that a mere handful of dies shared between four moneyers sufficed to strike the whole of York's contribution.

Seen in retrospect the coins underline neatly the real turning-point in the fortunes of Scandinavian York, the Hiberno-Norse intervention in the second decade of the 10th century. Paradoxically the alien acted as a catalyst towards integration—Ragnall's 920 submission to Edward the Elder was essentially a recognition that York was part of England. Seen only too clearly by the outsider was the political reality. Neither Denmark nor Norway was in a position to continue to flood any part of the Anglo-Celtic Isles with superfluous manpower, and the grandsons of Ívarr of Dublin knew only too well how agonizingly the barrel had had to be scraped to bring together the motley adventurers who restored the Norse presence in Ireland at a time when many must have written it off as a spent force. Just as a century and a half later Norman William detached England from Greater Scandinavia, so *c* 915 Norse Ragnall severed York from a Continental dream, and it is the coins that make the point. With the Hiberno-Norse intervention the coinage of York becomes essentially English, first of all in fabric and later in its very types. The interlopers had injected a measured dose of insular realism, and one may suspect that it was one founded on commercial interest. Few Norsemen were without a mercantile streak, and it can be no coincidence that names of men of Irish descent continue to be found among the York moneyers as late as the reign of Edward the Confessor—a feature of mixed marriages between Norse and Irish was the influence of the latter on the nomenclature of the offspring. A proportion at least of the 'strong-arm' men who gave Ragnall political credibility in the leadership crisis after Tettenhall may be supposed to have settled down almost overnight and become solid pillars of York's burgeoning commercial community.

The Dubliners themselves proved to be instinctive traders, and the incidence of the imported coins in Mr A B Ó Ríordáin's momentous excavations reveals that what was happening at York was part of a wider pattern, even though at Dublin a mint was not opened until the very end of the 10th century—perhaps in the late summer of 997. If we assume, then, that early 10th century York already partook of the nature of an emporium, the mercantile interest, Danish and Norse with an English and perhaps Frisian substratum which we ignore at our peril, must have found common ground in viewing political instability with something more than dismay. York wished to have a very real stake in markets west of the Pennines as well as south of the Humber, and the reconciliation of these on the surface discrepant objectives probably explains much that is seemingly inconsistent in York attitudes towards the house of Ívarr and Eric Haraldsson alike. To put it in terms which a majority of the Anglo-Danish population would certainly have understood, York knew on which side its bread was buttered—or should we say smørred?

Note

The text of the foregoing will be found essentially to conform to that of M Dolley, *Viking Coins of the Danelaw and of Dublin* (London 1965), with the occasional alteration of attribution and of emphasis to take account of research, not all of it as yet published, during the intervening period. The illustrations are adapted from certain of the figures on plates VIII and X of the late Sir Charles Oman's *Coinage of England* (Oxford 1931), an often underrated work but the one which came nearest to an understanding of the true sequence of the issues of 939-954 before the definitive work of the 1950s and 1960s, and these figures in turn go back to the monumental 19th century works of Rogers Ruding and Edward Hawkins. The 1965 booklet includes still serviceable notes on works for further reading, but on the historical side there must be added A P Smyth, *Scandinavian York and Dublin* (Dublin 1975), even if one or two points of detail are unlikely to command the assent of older established workers in the field.

The topography of Anglo-Scandinavian York   *R A Hall*

At the beginning of a paper which is concerned with the physical characteristics of Anglo-Scandinavian York— York, that is, between the years 876 and 1069—it is necessary to stress two points. The first is simply that in approaching the city's topography at this period, we are not dealing with an unchanging, 'frozen' townscape, but with one which may have been continually changing in much of its minor detail, and also perhaps in some of its major facets. The second point is that our knowledge of York at this period is peculiarly small, and that this paper can, in the main, only offer tentative conclusions or highlight topics where further research is required.

The majority of relevant excavations have been undertaken in the last quarter of a century, and their results have been intermittently synthesized in a disparate series of general studies of Viking-age York, which have catalogued and interpreted the evidence as it has become available. The earliest of these, by Waterman (1959), set a pattern for succeeding work in its treatment of a number of diverse strands of evidence. It drew a two-dimensional picture of the Anglo-Scandinavian city, plotting its extent in terms of the distribution firstly of objects broadly dated to this era, and secondly of street-names recorded in the 12th century which might be of pre-Conquest origin. The small but important group of contemporary or near-contemporary documentary references was also referred to in order to provide a background for the other evidence. It is a salutary reminder of the infancy of post-Roman oriented excavation in York to contrast Waterman's absence of references to secular buildings within the city with his detailed descriptions of a large body of material salvaged by chance during road-making and building work.

This has been followed by *Anglian and Viking York* (Cramp 1967), an essay on pre-Norman York by Ramm (1972), and a preface on the subject in Volume IV of the Royal Commission on Historical Monuments' inventory of York. In addition, Radley (1971) has contributed a more specialist paper, concentrating on one small area of the city in the vicinity of Ousegate, Coppergate, and Pavement.

All these studies were written before the inception of York Archaeological Trust in 1972, which since that time has pursued a policy of rescue and research excavation on sites threatened by redevelopment within the city, as well as collecting whatever information becomes available in non-archaeological excavation work. As a result, it is now possible to challenge some of the assumptions made previously about the Anglo-Scandinavian city, to understand more fully some of the difficulties noted by earlier commentators, and also to add a relatively large amount of new archaeological information.

A major influence on both the general and particular development of the Viking-age town was the remains of its Roman and Anglian predecessors. Their growth in turn had been partly determined by natural factors, and its geographical and geological setting had made the vicinity a focus for activity from at least the Neolithic period (Radley 1974). The city is situated on a well-drained ridge of moraine running from east to west across the Vale of York, at the point where it is pierced by the tidal head of the River Ouse. It is thus an excellent centre of communications, to its hinterland both by way of the moraine ridge and along the tributary River Foss, or to the north-eastern English coast and beyond via the River Ouse.

There may have been a farming community settled hereabouts during the Iron Age (Radley 1974, 12-13), but presumably for reasons of defence the Roman military command made its headquarters between the rivers Ouse and Foss. A 20.23 hectare (50 acre) legionary fortress was constructed here, and ultimately fortified with stone walls whose south-western facade incorporated projecting interval towers. Extra-mural development took place along the Ouse frontage and on the spit at the rivers' confluence, and there is also evidence for a fortified enclosure of some 200m² extending from the west corner to the north-west gate of the fortress (RCHMY I, 45-7).

A bridge crossed the River Ouse at a point opposite the modern Guildhall and led to the civilian town, which was eventually granted the status of *colonia*. This too was defended—the medieval city wall is known to have followed and extended its western wall—but the precise location of the south-eastern walls is a matter for conjecture. Since the distribution of Roman material is sparse at the east end of the medieval enclosure, it may be that this extends further than its Roman predecessor did, although uneven recording of data might also be the cause of this apparent inequality.

As will be seen, excavation has shown that individual Roman buildings were upstanding for many centuries after the Roman withdrawal but, in the face of an almost total absence of excavated material of 5th, 6th, or early 7th century date, there has been much speculation concerning the fate of the city as a whole in the immediate post-Roman centuries.

It has been suggested (Faull 1974, 24-5) that the city remained in British hands throughout the 5th century, was taken by the Anglo-Saxons by *c* 575, but developed only in the reign of Edwin (616-32). It has also been thought that occupation may have been confined by extensive flooding in the 5th and 6th centuries which rendered large low-lying tracts of the town uninhabitable (Ramm 1971, 181-3). However, there has been no evidence from recent excavations to support this latter theory, and critical examination of the evidence adduced in its support suggests that some of it at least has lent itself to misinterpretation (see p 70). For example, the record of 'warp' (an alluvial deposit) being found below High Ousegate and Coppergate (Benson 1902, 64) is almost certainly incorrect, the deposits being in fact typical early medieval rubbish layers incorporating much organic material (Hall 1976b).

Even from the Christian Anglian period (*c* 650-850) finds of any sort are a rarity, because there was little or no locally produced pottery in use at this period. The picture which previous writers have drawn, and one which has been confirmed in several recent excavations, is of layers of silt and debris collecting to a depth of up to half a metre on and over the Roman streets. These layers contain only Roman material, but their depth and nature make it unlikely that they accumulated during the Roman period. An analogous discovery was a pit on the Blake Street site which was rich in Roman pottery but which also contained a coin of Eanred (*c* 810-*c* 841).

Nonetheless, historical sources indicate that in the Christian Anglian period York had a flourishing monastic school and another major church, the enigmatic *Alma Sophia*. Sculptural fragments from a number of other sites point to additional churches, among them, for example, St Mary Bishophill Junior. There is, too, a body of evidence for international trade being channelled via York, and there was certainly contact with the Rhineland, which was perhaps conducted by the Frisian merchants known to have resided in the city. Yet the larger ecclesiastical establishments and the commercial activity do not necessarily imply a large population in the pre-Viking town, and the paucity of archaeological evidence for secular structures of this date does nothing to contradict this viewpoint. Only its defences suggest, by their scale, that Anglian York was perhaps a major settlement as well as an important focal point. Evidence for an Anglian defensive circuit has so far come from only one site, approximately 75m north of the Multangular Tower. Here, behind York City Library, the late Jeffrey Radley and Mr B K Davison have between them uncovered the remains of perhaps three or four phases of post-Roman and pre-Viking embankment (Webster & Cherry 1972, 165-7), the most spectacular component of which is the so-called Anglian tower, which plugs a breach in the Roman wall (Radley 1971). These embankments demonstrate that someone or some group of people had sufficient interest in York to expend much time and labour on providing for its continued defence, and suggest that there may have been a static population of some size, rather than just a handful of clerics and a small trading community.

Whatever the size of the Anglian town, it seems from the known distribution of Viking-age finds (Fig 20) that the Anglo-Scandinavian period was one of expansion for the city, and it has recently been suggested that 'York was one of the greatest North Sea trading places of the Viking age and probably excelled them all in size' (Biddle 1976, 123). In the fortress area it seems that the line of the Roman walls continued to delineate part of the defended area. Evidence has again come from Davison's excavations on the north-west side of the fortress (Webster & Cherry 1972, 165-7), where an earthen rampart capped by a timber palisade has been assigned to the time of the Vikings' capture of the city, and may perhaps be linked with Asser's assertion that the city was refortified by its new lords.

A recent interpretation of sections cut by S N Miller in 1925-7 immediately east of the north corner of the fortress and immediately north of its east corner, whose principal aim was to examine the development of the Roman defences and which only show post-Roman stratigraphy in outline, has suggested that layers which may correspond to that recognized more positively by Davison can be isolated (Radley 1971, 37-8), and demonstrates that the limits of the fortified area remained constant here from the Roman period.

However, the south-east and south-west sides of the Roman fortress defences have not survived above ground, and it is not known when they became indefensible or redundant. The west corner tower of the fortress (the Multangular Tower) has Roman masonry still surviving to a height of 5.80m and there is no indication that there was any need to add to the Roman defences here in the pre-Conquest period, since the ground beyond the fortress falls steeply away to the River Ouse. The two adjacent Roman interval towers on the south-western defences are at and just below modern ground surface, and because of this no evidence for their fate has survived more recent activities in their vicinities. Further to the east, however, Roman remains have been covered by an increasingly thick build-up of post-Roman deposits, so that the foundation of the southern corner tower of the fortress is approximately 3.10m below the modern surface.

Debris may possibly have started to accumulate against the Roman fortress walls soon after the departure of the legions, as it certainly did in and after the 9th century, but again the absence of datable artefacts belonging to the period *c* 450-850 makes certainty difficult. Thus in excavations against the south corner tower of the fortress at 12 Feasegate, Stead encountered deposits abutting approximately the lowest 1m of the wall which contained only atypical groups of Roman pottery, most probably residual in nature and attributable in their collection as groups to the post-Roman period (Stead 1958, 522-3 and Fig 3).

The north-east side of the fortress wall has been seen to survive to heights of approximately 3m in several excavations, and layers of 9th-11th century date have been seen to have accumulated against its outer face at heights ranging from 1 to 3m above its base (Dyer & Wenham 1958, 424 and Fig 2; Wenham 1968, 165). Normally these layers provide merely a *terminus post quem* for the robbing of the wall, more precise dating evidence for which has usually been removed by modern disturbance. However, at 1-2 King's Square, Stead (1968, 154 and Fig 3) was able to demonstrate that robbing of the ashlar outer face had

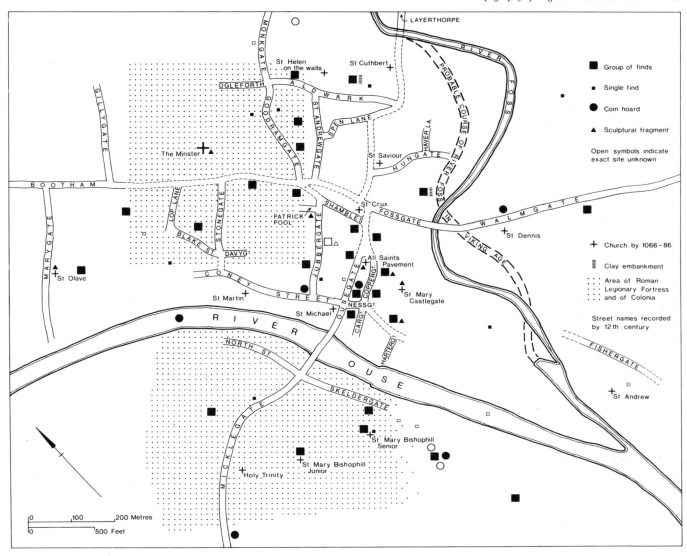

Fig 20   Distribution of evidence for the topography, economy, and environment of Anglo-Scandinavian York. The course of the River Foss is hypothetical, based on information in RCHMY 1, 64-5

occurred either during the Anglian or early in the Anglo-Scandinavian period, and it is possible that robbing of the upper parts of the wall also occurred elsewhere along this side of the fortress in the late pre-Conquest period. Certainly by c 1200 virtually all traces of the wall right down to and including its foundations had been removed at Bedern (Addyman 1975b, 2).

The rising ground surface did not lead to a strengthening of the defensive circuit here as it did on the north-west side of the fortress, and indeed the evidence for robbing clearly shows the defensive line being actively dismantled. Rather, by the later 9th or 10th century, the town seems to have extended to the south-east into a formerly extra-mural area, and there is some evidence that an embankment was erected to complement the natural defences provided in this area by the rivers.

The first indication of this came in 1950 when a 20m length of embankment running north-east to south-west and dated to the 9th-10th centuries was discovered at Hungate (Richardson 1959, 59-65). It seemed to be part of a major scheme of land reclamation and drainage which also

involved the laying of thick layers of brushwood and the construction of a series of gulleys. The embankment itself survived to a height of up to 2m and consisted of layers of clay and brushwood, pinned together with stakes. No trace of any military features such as a stockade was found along its top, and the embankment is most likely to represent an attempt to prevent the River Foss from flooding. The Foss is thought, on the basis of the discovery of Roman wharves to the west of the present channel, to have run further in that direction at this point than it does today.

The Hungate embankment was linked by its excavator with a 'wickerwork stockade' found in 1902 below 25-27 High Ousegate (Benson 1902). This stood up to 2.45m in height and ran from the north-north-east to the south-south-west at the Coppergate end of the property. Although some recent commentators have interpreted this find as evidence for part of a pre-Conquest city boundary, a recent small excavation astride the recorded line of the 'stockade' revealed only a relatively flimsy alignment of stakes comparable to property boundaries encountered during other archaeological work in the city, and the idea of a major defensive line here may be abandoned (Hall 1976b).

However, work by York Excavation Group on a site in Aldwark, opposite a dog-leg in the medieval city wall, has revealed a clay feature over 6m wide and 1.2m high, built over silty deposits and dated to the pre-Conquest period (*Interim* Vol 2 no 4, 21-5). The kink in the medieval wall suggests that there was once a boundary of some sort demarcated from this point, and comparison of the form, composition, and date of the Hungate and Aldwark features suggests that both may well have been a part of the same Anglo-Scandinavian period civic reorganization. If this hypothesis is accepted, the course of the embankment's expected continuation still remains a mystery, as is the precise course of the River Foss, which probably influenced it.

Wherever the precise limits of settlement in the area were defined, there is no doubt that Ousegate, Coppergate, and Pavement were the main streets through this quarter of the city, and it has been suggested that the focus of commercial activity was at their junction (Radley 1971, 39). Their importance was inevitable since Ousegate led directly from Ouse Bridge, which had replaced the former Roman bridge approximately 260m upstream at an unknown date in the 5th-9th centuries. Virtually no new information has become available about the minor elements in the street pattern of this area, although the discovery of 13th century wooden structures well in advance of the modern pavement line in Coppergate may be taken to infer that the Viking-age street was also considerably narrower than its modern counterpart (Hall 1976b).

It was largely the efforts of Radley in rescuing information during building work in Ousegate and Pavement which refocused attention on the importance of this vicinity in the Anglo-Scandinavian period, and small excavations by York Archaeological Trust at 5 Coppergate and 6-8 Pavement have both added to the large collection of pre-Conquest material from the area. This wealth of objects contrasts markedly with the paltry collection from the area of the Roman fortress, but this should not lead us to the conclusion that the majority of this latter area was inexplicably deserted in a total move to the Ouse-Foss confluence. Quite large sectors of the fortress, notably in the north-east quadrant, have not been subject to any modern redevelopment, and this must partially explain the lack of Anglo-Scandinavian finds. Another reason for their absence has been demonstrated in recent excavations at 9 Blake Street, 21 Davygate, and 1-5 Aldwark, where at widely separated sites the same phenomenon of 13th century levels directly overlying late Roman structures has been observed (Addyman 1975b, 8; Addyman 1976a, 10). This argues for a major clearance undertaken perhaps *c* 1200, which removed nearly all traces of Anglo-Scandinavian period occupation. The only exception is the important discovery of a Scandinavian-style trefoil brooch mould and contemporary pre-Conquest pottery in a pit dug into Roman levels on the Blake Street site. Thus while Radley's statement that no large area of domestic remains has yet been excavated within the fortress still holds true (1971, 54), it is now possible to appreciate more fully the reason for this. The view that the place name King's Court/King's Square points to a Viking-age royal palace centred about the *porta principalis sinistra* (Ramm 1974, 248-9) and the siting of the forerunner of the present Minster, as yet attested only by a part of its 11th century graveyard (Pattison 1973; 211-5; Phillips 1975, 24), also indicate that the fortress area remained an important part of the pre-Conquest city.

Yet although this area housed the archiepiscopal church, and possibly a Viking-age royal palace, the later pre-Conquest earls are thought to have had their residence in an enclave corresponding to the Roman enclosure off the west corner of the fortress, in the area later occupied by St Mary's Abbey. The principal evidence for this is again a place name, *Earlsburgh*, recorded in the 18th century as referring to the vicinity of Marygate (Waterman 1959, 66), but it may also be conjectured that St Olave's church in Marygate, built by Siward during his tenure of the earldom, was designed as a private church within the grounds of the earl's residence.

Also north of the Ouse but at the opposite end of the city, east of the Foss, lies the Walmgate area. Knowledge of its origin and growth has increased little in recent years, and the main evidence for activity here in the Anglo-Scandinavian period remains the unstratified groups of chance finds and the sculptural fragments noted by Waterman (1959, Fig 4), which cluster by the side of Walmgate, the main route out of York towards the north-east. It remains a major research priority to learn through excavation whether or not the medieval walls here overlie a pre-Conquest defence.

This question is also unanswered in respect of the city walls south of the Ouse. Here in the area of the former *colonia* the medieval wall perpetuates in at least one length the Roman alignment (RCHMY I, 49), but it is not known if there were intermediary refurbishings of the defences between these two major constructional phases. The principal street in this area, Micklegate, veers markedly from the Roman grid in its course down the morainic ridge to the Ouse bridge-head, and inside the defences there seems little evidence for continuity in major elements of the *colonia*'s topography.

Immediately north of the church of St Mary Bishophill Junior, excavations by L P Wenham have revealed that in the late Anglian or early Anglo-Scandinavian period a fish-processing factory was in operation here within a ruinous Roman house. By the early 10th century the area had become a graveyard, into which inhumations accompanied by grave goods were placed (Wilson & Hurst 1963, 312). Final publication of the results is still awaited, but the available data suggest that the 10th century was a crucial time in the development of this property, a time when changes occurred which determined the function of the site as churchyard down to the present day.

Anglo-Scandinavian period reworking of the Roman topography is also attested at a site on the corner of Bishophill and Carr's Lane. Excavation by York Archaeological Trust in 1973 showed that Roman building remains here had been totally robbed out during the 9th-11th centuries, but unfortunately later medieval activity had removed any evidence for the Anglo-Scandinavian layout (Carver 1976).

A degree of continuity from the Roman period onwards can, however, be recognized on a site immediately to the south-east of the 1973 excavation. Here a 4th century house may have served as the nucleus for a 10th century church of St Mary Bishophill Senior: although no structural remains of this have been discovered, a church of intermediate date between the Roman structure and the recently demolished 11th century church may be conjectured to account for the correspondence in width between the Roman and 11th century structures, since the Roman layout was largely unknown to the 11th century builders. A disturbed grave containing an early 10th century strap-end may be taken to provide a little extra weight to the argument for such a church. A more obvious survival was the north-east wall of the Roman house, which stood to a height

Plate VIII 16-22 Coppergate, York: vertical view of three late 10th-11th century buildings (photo: M S Duffy)

Plate IX 16-22 Coppergate, York: oblique view of late 10th-11th century building (photo: M S Duffy)

of over 1.1m into the 12th century, serving as a part of the enclosure wall for the 11th century church (Ramm 1976, 45-7).

Evidence for both continuity and discontinuity in Roman features has come from an excavation down the slope from the sites just mentioned. On a site in the corner of Carr's Lane and Skeldergate, it was found that the remains of Roman structures immediately below the upper plateau had been partially levelled to provide the platform for a timber building, probably in the 8th century. However, since the Roman structures were not investigated in detail it is not possible to assess the degree of concordance between the Roman and post-Roman structures. Only one wall of pre-Conquest date definitely shared its alignment with a Roman feature, a riverside road, but this coincidence may be due to both having been laid out with respect to the river, rather than one directly influencing the other (Bishop 1976).

Unequivocal evidence was, however, forthcoming at the Skeldergate site to demonstrate that tenement boundaries existing in the Anglo-Scandinavian period were perpetuated into the 18th century, and this introduces the topic of the individual properties which constituted the city. Domesday Book records that in 1066 there were 1607 inhabited dwellings in six of the city's shires, with no figures provided for the seventh. What their size was, what these properties consisted of, and how they would have appeared to contemporary observers is almost impossible to answer.

Radley (1971, 45) suggested that the modern property lines in High Ousegate indicate an average medieval tenement width of about 5.5m, laid out originally in the pre-Conquest period. Recent excavations at 6-8 Pavement (Addyman & Harrison 1975) and 16-22 Coppergate have produced additional indications that this was so, but it is also clear (*pace* Radley 1971, 42; see Radley's Fig 8, p 44), that the excavations at the High Ousegate/Parliament Street corner revealed two structures on diverging alignments. Another example of Anglo-Scandinavian period structures with diverging alignments, only this time related to a more obvious chronological separation, was recorded below 5 Coppergate in 1902 (Benson 1902, Pl III), and it seems that there was a replanning of the property boundaries in this area at least in the two hundred years before the Norman Conquest.

The overall layout of individual properties must have varied as natural and pre-existing topographical features will have hindered a regular development, and there is no firm indication of how messuages were utilized. Benson's report on his 1902 watching brief suggests that one enormous structure stretched almost 27.5m between High Ousegate and Coppergate, whilst the work at Skeldergate (Bishop 1976) showed small pre-Conquest buildings spread over one messuage. All other previous excavations have only discovered small parts of structures which cannot be related to the totality of the messuage.

Because of the patchy nature of the evidence only tentative remarks can be made about the vernacular building traditions of Anglo-Scandinavian York, but at present it seems possible to distinguish two main groups of wall-building techniques. In the first, withes are woven around uprights of varying size and shape and then plastered with a coat of daub. Walls constructed in this way have been encountered in excavations at 6-8 Pavement (Addyman & Harrison 1975, 221 and Fig 12), and on the basis of finds at the High Ousegate/Parliament Street corner and 5 Coppergate it seems that property boundaries were delineated with similar walls without the daub coating.

Characteristic of the second group of techniques is the use of horizontally laid planks, supported internally by uprights. Both uprights and horizontal members may either rest directly in a trenched foundation, as was the case with a building partially revealed at 1-2 King's Square (Stead 1968, 154), or be seated on or in a sill beam, as at 1 Parliament Street (Radley 1971, 42). Often only a sill beam survives, as at 25-27 High Ousegate (Benson 1902, 64), 65 Low Petergate (Wenham 1972, 76) or the Carr's Lane/Skeldergate corner (Bishop 1976), and even in the other two instances quoted above only 0.15-0.20m of planked superstructure survived. This emphasizes the importance of current excavations at 16-22 Coppergate in which horizontally laid plank walls and their upright supports survive to heights of up to 1.20m and 1.80m respectively above their sill foundations (Plates VIII and IX).

The Norman attempts between 1067 and 1069 to exert dominance over Anglo-Scandinavian York resulted in topographical changes throughout the city, a physical manifestation of the new political order. Twin mottes were thrown up at the east of the city, facing each other across the River Ouse. Domesday Book says that in doing this one of the city's seven shires was wasted. Local reaction was to welcome the Anglo-Danish counter-invasion of 1069, and in a pre-emptive response to this the Norman garrison of York burned part of the city. This was an obvious and major disruption in civic life, and Domesday Book again makes it clear that in 1086 over half of the houses in the city were still unoccupied.

One structure whose rebuilding soon began was the Minster, which Archbishop Thomas of Bayeux realigned on a liturgically correct east-west orientation. This was at odds with the surviving alignment of the main streets of Roman origin nearby, and also, if the orientation of the recently-discovered 11th century graves is a reliable guide, with the alignment of the pre-Conquest Minster. Not long afterwards, in 1088, York's other major medieval religious establishment, St Mary's Abbey, was granted land in the vicinity of Earlsburgh, and put a large area here to a new ecclesiastical use. Thus both in destruction and innovation the two decades following the Norman Conquest mark a clear divide between the distinct Anglo-Scandinavian and medieval topographies of York.

Note

This contribution is largely based on the work of the York Archaeological Trust since 1972. Thanks are due for permission to make preliminary publication in advance of the definitive reports in *The Archaeology of York*.

Industry and commerce in Anglo-Scandinavian York

Arthur MacGregor

Introduction

The strategic position which first recommended the site of present-day York to the Roman military command also ensured its subsequent survival as the major commercial clearing house for the entire north-east of England. It lies on an elevated land route (see p 31) which has probably been an important commercial thoroughfare since at least the Bronze Age (Radley 1974, 12). The River Ouse and its lesser tributary, the Foss, also had enormous commercial significance, providing in the case of the Ouse a direct line of communication to the North Sea, and in that of the Foss a sheltered anchorage off the flood-prone course of the larger river. And finally, the route westwards through the hinterland towards the Irish Sea, seen by Radley (1974) as the high road along which passed a considerable amount of prehistoric Irish trade, took on an important new significance with the establishment of Scandinavian kingdoms based on Dublin in 841 and on York a generation later in 876.

Relations between York and the emporia of north-western Europe had been well established for some considerable period of time before the arrival at the city gates of the *micel here*. A certain amount of indirect historical evidence can be mustered for this claim: Alcuin, for example, speaks of York as *emporium terrae commune marisque* (Raine, J, 1879, 350), while Altfrid's *Life of St Liudger* (composed before 849) alludes to the presence of a community of Frisian merchants in the city (Whitelock 1955, 724-5). Far from extinguishing this contact with the European mainland, the implanting of a Danish society in York and the subsequent recognition of the city as the capital of the Danelaw immensely increased the scope of its contacts, the Scandinavian north and the Baltic littoral being added to and perhaps to some degree supplanting intercourse with the Low Countries. Some measure of continuity might have been encouraged by links already established between the incoming Scandinavians and the Frisians: it may be noted, for example, that the three leaders of the Great Army are described in the *Annals of Lindisfarne* as *duces Dani et Frisonum*, while one of their number (Ubba) is designated *dux Fresonum* (Pertz 1866, 506).

By around the year 1000, however, an anonymous *Life of St Oswald* describes York as populated with some 30,000 adults and being 'filled with the treasures of merchants, chiefly of the Danish race' (*maxime ex Danorum gente*) (Raine 1879, 454), perhaps indicating a major new commercial alignment as well as reflecting a new ethnic bias in the city's population.

Archaeological evidence of contact between York and the continent in the period immediately prior to the Scandinavian conquest is exceedingly thin, definite imports being limited to a few sherds of Tating ware found recently at Skeldergate (Addyman 1976b, 29). An early find in York of coins from the Dorestad mint (Dolley 1966b, 1-7) may be noted in this context, while reciprocal evidence from the continental mainland includes the discovery at Dorestad of a silver *sceat* of a type generally thought to have been minted at York (Dr D H Hill, pers comm). One or two artefacts from recent excavations in York could conceivably be Frisian rather than Scandinavian in inspiration (if not in origin): among these may be included a comb fragment (Fig 29, 5), which finds an exact parallel in Dorestad (Roes 1965, 62, Pl XXVIII, 216), and a leather boot (Fig 34, 1) which, although of a type found fairly commonly in Anglo-Scandinavian York (see p 53 below); is derived from a pattern ultimately of Frisian origin (cf Hald 1972, 98). The adoption of many Frisian traits (including the method of shoemaking involved here) by Scandinavian craftsmen, together with the difficulties of precise archaeological dating, makes it impossible to be certain whether these articles arrived before or soon after the period of Scandinavian settlement.

Anglo-Scandinavian commerce: the archaeological evidence

Despite the historical evidence for flourishing international commerce, the material remains of any such activity are scarce indeed and their true significance difficult to evaluate. Many aspects of the material culture of York described below are wholly Scandinavian in flavour, but with the wholesale settlement of Scandinavian immigrants which took place in the later 9th and 10th centuries, this is no more than should be expected and, considering the evidence for local industries outlined below, there is no reason to doubt that the vast majority of these objects were manufactured locally. In order that non-local products of everyday character can be recognized, however, they must generally bear some distinctive and exclusive appearance or be made in materials which are locally unavailable. Under this latter category, six groups are discussed below; a seventh group, comprising ornaments made of amber, certainly formed the basis of a thriving manufacturing industry in York (p 40-1), but whether the raw material was imported in bulk from the Baltic (where it occurs prolifically) or whether, as seems more likely, it was gathered no further away than the Yorkshire coast (where it is occasionally washed up), cannot be proven. The evidence from jet (p 40-1) and pottery (p 56-7) should also be noted in this context.

1. *Steatite*

From the Lloyds Bank, 6-8 Pavement, excavations (Addyman 1975a, 218-24) came two body fragments from steatite (soapstone) bowls (Fig 21, 1-2), one of them with a plain rim and the other apparently incorporating a raised cordon. These seem to be the first steatite objects of this period to have been found in England[1] and the very restricted distribution of natural deposits of this material demand that it must have been imported. Steatite was commonly used in the Norse homeland for the production of bowls and other vessels and a flourishing export trade

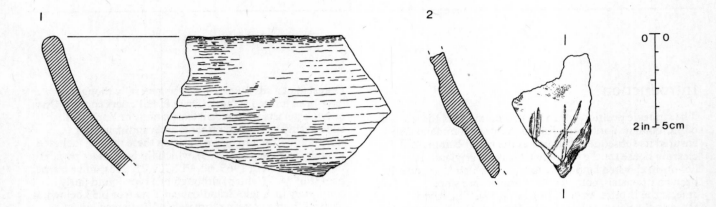

Fig 21   Steatite bowl fragments, 6-8 Pavement. Scale 1:2

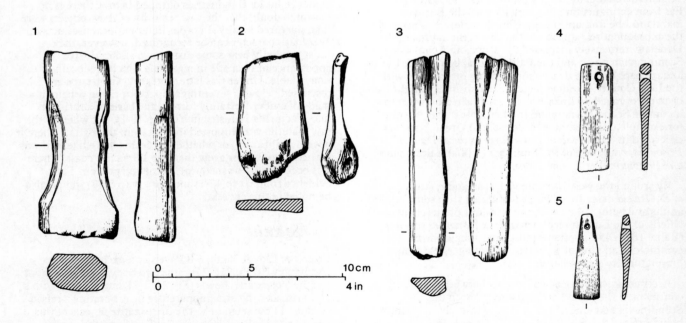

Fig 22   Honestones: 1: sandstone, 6-8 Pavement; 2-3 schist, 6-8 Pavement; 4: schist, 5 Coppergate; 5: schist, Skeldergate. Scale 1:2

was developed with Denmark and northern Germany (Skjølsvold 1961, 149-56). Norwegian settlers in northern Scotland brought this technology with them but exploited local sources; these deposits are extremely limited in distribution, however, and with the exception of a few minor outcrops elsewhere (Hamilton 1962, 71) are effectively restricted to the Shetland Isles, where intensive exploitation of certain quarries has been demonstrated for the Viking period (Hamilton 1956, 206-10). Geological thin-sectioning of the York fragments[2] has revealed that they both compare satisfactorily with material from the Cunningsburgh (Shetland) quarries, although in view of the distinct possibility of direct importation from Norway it might be unwise to draw too firm conclusions from this fact until a Scandinavian origin can be categorically disproved. Evidence from both the Norwegian and Shetland quarries indicates that the rough shaping of vessels was carried out on site (and was, indeed, an integral part of the quarrying process, since the outer profile of each bowl was hewn on the living rock before the individual units were detached). Whether these two bowls were brought to York in the finished state or whether they were traded as roughouts cannot be demonstrated; either is possible. Deposits of carbon on the outer surfaces and striations suggesting repeated scouring with sand imply that they were probably used as cooking vessels.

2.　*Mayen lava*

The trade in quernstones made from the vessicular lava of the Mayen series has a long prehistoric ancestry (Crawford *et al* 1955, 68-76). In the Anglo-Saxon period it seems that Dorestad probably played an important part in the northerly distribution of these querns, but they continued to reach centres such as Thetford into the 11th and 12th centuries (Dunning 1956, 220-1).

Several fragments of lava querns have now been found on excavations in York, although most are from early medieval levels. Some were noted at 6-8 Pavement[3], however, and serve to demonstrate a continuity of contact in the Anglo-Scandinavian period, a situation confirmed by the occurrence at the same excavations of Pingsdorf-type ware, probably from a similar geographical source (see below).

3.　*Honestones*

Ellis's study of the petrography and provenance of certain honestones (Ellis 1969) has added an important new dimension to the range of demonstrable contacts between England and the Scandinavian north. Ellis has shown that many representatives of the 'schist hone' series, first appearing in England in contexts dating to the early phases of Scandinavian settlement, can be traced to a source area in southern Norway. The well-known quarries at Eidsborg, Telemark, have provided excellent matching samples for some of the hones found in England. Several examples from York are listed by Ellis (1969, 137, 144) and others have been recovered from 6-8 Pavement, and 5 Coppergate[4] (Fig 22). Clearly, schist hones have formed the basis of a very extensive trade across the North Sea. Interestingly, the remains of a ship which sank while carrying a cargo of these hones has been found at Klåstad Vestfold (Christensen 1970, 21-4) and, while this particular vessel seems to have been engaged on a purely local voyage—the excavator suggests that it *may* have been bound for Kaupang—it demonstrates vividly the actuality of seaborne trade in this material.

The Norwegian suppliers had no monopoly, however, on the English market: of eleven hones from 6-8 Pavement, eight were of Norse origin and three were of Millstone Grit, probably from the Pennines; perhaps they performed complementary functions, the Millstone Grit being used in the initial sharpening and the schist hones producing a fine cutting edge.

4.　*Pottery*

Imported pottery has been recovered on two occasions from layers of Anglo-Scandinavian date in York; in both instances the fragments were body sherds only, but from their hard, cream-coloured fabric and red-painted decoration they could be identified as 'Pingsdorf-type' wares. The Hungate excavations produced a single sherd of this ware, found among brushwood levels underlying the clay bank (Richardson 1959, 79), while more recently from 6-8 Pavement came two more fragments (Holdsworth, forthcoming). It would be premature, particularly in view of the range of possible sources (Hurst 1969b, 93-147) and the absence, as yet, of any mineralogical analyses of the York sherds, to claim any more precise categorization, but an origin in the Rhineland seems most probable.

5.　*Ivory*

Two kinds of ivory may be considered here, although the implications they carry in terms of trade are quite different: they derive from the walrus and the elephant respectively.

Ohthere (or Ottar), a Norwegian mariner who visited the court of King Alfred and whose tales were interpolated in Alfred's translation of Orosius's *History of the World*, was one of those who pursued the walrus for its ivory: he reported that he travelled as far as the North Cape, 'chiefly . . . for the walruses, for they have very fine ivory in their tusks . . . and their hide is very good for ship's cables' (reproduced in Jones 1968, 159). Although there have been a number of sightings on British shores in recent years and although its former distribution may have extended somewhat further south (King, J E, 1964, 38), the walrus is predominantly an Arctic animal and the bulk of the ivory utilized in the British Isles would have been imported.

Although considerable quantities were used in England for the manufacture of devotional and ornamental objects (cf Beckwith 1972, 116), the only walrus ivory so far found in York—a seal matrix inscribed *SIG SNARRI THEOLENARII* (The Seal of Snarr, the Toll Gatherer)— seems to be of late 12th century date and therefore falls outside the chronological scope of this survey. Nonetheless, it seems likely that York would have functioned as a major clearing house for imported walrus ivory from Norway and elsewhere; an implement of morse ivory from Bramham, West Yorkshire (Kendrick 1935, 339-40), may be noted in this context.

Two fragments of elephant ivory were found by Radley in an Anglo-Scandinavian or Norman context during excavation in 1969-70 on the city defences (Radley 1972, 50, 64). The contacts which they indicate are clearly with the south rather than the north, although any such contact is likely to have been limited in nature and may in any case have been at second or third hand. The ivory fragments in question were, however, judged (*ibid*) to have been broken in the course of manufacture, so that local utilization of imported raw material is obviously implied.

6. *Silk*

The evidence for a thriving textile industry in York is outlined and recent finds of woollen cloth as well as linen are referred to below (p 56). One textile fragment, however, stands out as an undoubted import, for it is made of silk. This piece was recovered during excavations at 5 Coppergate, where it was found together with remnants of coarse woollen cloth and other remains in a context dated broadly to the Anglo-Scandinavian period. The Coppergate fragment—possibly part of a head-dress—is discussed in a report by Mr John Hedges, which deals with all contemporary textile remains from York and is to be published in MacGregor, forthcoming. It is sufficient to note here that the silk has obviously been imported, conceivably from China but much more probably from one of the Mediterranean production centres: by the 10th century, Byzantine silk manufacture had been extended from the east Mediterranean to southern Italy (Guillou 1974, 92 ff; 1976, 69-84) and by that time a thriving industry had already been developed under Islamic control in Spain (Guillou 1976, 71 ff). While there was, therefore, considerable scope for direct maritime contact with these production centres in the Mediterranean, the possibility of a Frisian agency in the introduction of this silk cannot be ruled out (cf Jellema 1955, 26, note 39). Alternatively, the silk could have been transmitted to northern Europe via the Russian river systems, as has been postulated for a number of silk fragments found at Birka (Geijer 1938, 64-7).

These six groups of material, plus the evidence of coins, which are considered elsewhere (p 26ff), are all we have to demonstrate physically the long-range commercial contacts of the merchants of Viking-age York. While some, such as the hones and the lava querns, are undoubtedly the products of commercial intercourse, others such as the single silk fragment and the pieces of steatite are impossible to interpret at present: whether they prove to be the first of many finds indicating frequent commercial exchange or whether they are to be unique finds, perhaps casual souvenirs of an oversea voyage, only further excavation will decide. With present-day techniques of research and conservation, we may also be able to recover evidence of the more ephemeral classes of merchandise which are likely to have changed hands in the markets of York, such as hides, furs, and foodstuffs. In the latter category, a pre-Conquest fish processing plant discovered by Wenham at Bishophill (RCHMY 4, xxxv) is of especial interest.

In the meantime, a growing body of evidence is coming to light which demonstrates a range of manufacturing industries thriving within the city walls and, no doubt, supplying those same markets with the bulk of their merchandise. The following review will serve to illustrate York's other face, for as well as an emporium of international standing it was also a manufacturing centre of the first order.

Manufacturing industries in Anglo-Scandinavian York

In any review of this nature, the names of comparatively few excavations and even fewer excavators will necessarily be cited repeatedly, for present-day archaeological knowledge of Anglo-Scandinavian York rests on the researches of only a handful of workers active in the last century or so.

An early discovery was made in 1840, near St Margaret's Church, Walmgate, and included combs, pins, querns, and timber fragments (Raine, A, 1955, 100). More important finds, effectively unstratified but again mostly of Anglo-Scandinavian date, emerged during the construction of the Quaker Meeting House, Clifford Street, in 1884 (Yorkshire Museum, *Handbook to the Antiquities* (1891), 216-8). By 1902 George Benson was at hand to record something of the stratigraphy and structures as well as to catalogue the objects found at 25-7 High Ousegate (Benson 1902, 64-7) and, a few years later, repeated this service during building work at the corner of Castlegate and Coppergate (Benson 1906, 72-6).

During 1949-51, an area of the Anglo-Scandinavian city was laid bare while the foundations were dug for a telephone exchange at Hungate (Richardson 1959, 51-114) and yielded useful insights into various aspects of industrial practice (see below). Important stratified groups of material were recovered in 1956 from Feasegate by Dyer & Wenham (1958, 419-25) and Stead (1958, 515-38), while Wenham produced further useful information in 1963 from excavations in King's Square (Wenham 1968, 165-8). Two important surveys have already appeared which have dealt with aspects of the industrial activities carried on in Anglo-Scandinavian York: Waterman's study of small finds from this period (Waterman 1959, 59-105) remains a standard work of reference, while Radley's survey of earlier work, complemented by his own excavations at Barclay's Bank, 1 Parliament Street, and Lloyds' Bank, 2-4 Pavement (Radley 1971, 37-57) is full of useful factual information and stimulating speculation.

York Archaeological Trust, following the efforts of these scholars without whom our knowledge of Anglo-Scandinavian York would be slender indeed, has since its inception in 1972 been able to field a permanent excavating team which has on occasion concentrated its attentions on deposits of this period. Some reference to these excavations is made in interim reports published hitherto (Addyman 1975a, 200-31; 1976b, 1-32), while final reports will appear in *The Archaeology of York (AY)*, published as a series of fascicules for York Archaeological Trust by the Council for British Archaeology. The principal excavations by the Trust mentioned in the following text are those at Lloyds' Bank, 6-8 Pavement, which took place in 1972, and at 16-22 Coppergate, where they began in 1976 and are still in progress. A number of other sites (located in Fig 20) are also mentioned.

Amber and jet

Although neither amber nor jet is to be found in the immediate vicinity of York, numerous objects in these materials have been found in the city, some of them broken in the course of manufacture and clearly indicating that they were being worked on the spot. As already mentioned (p 57), it is conceivable that stocks of raw amber could have been brought directly from the Baltic or North German area for manufacture in York, but it seems more likely that fragments were gleaned from the beaches of the east coast where they are still washed up today. Since all (or nearly all) of this water-borne amber will have originated in the Baltic and will be indistinguishable from material deliberately collected there and subsequently shipped to England, it seems impossible to decide this issue one way or the other at the present time. Jet, on the other hand, would almost certainly have been brought from the shale beds exposed on the cliffs around Whitby and no question arises of its being imported from further afield: indeed, there was even a small-scale export trade in this material to Scandinavia (Shetelig 1944, 3-14), probably through York.

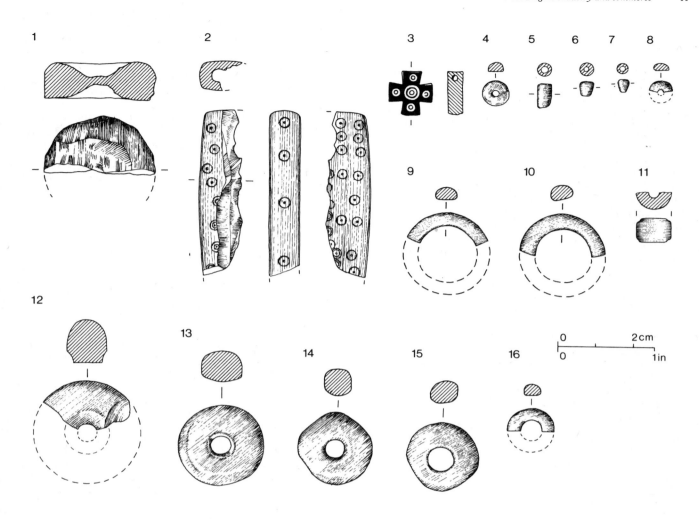

Fig 23   *Jet, glass, and amber. 1: jet bead rough-out, 6-8 Pavement; 2-3 jet ornaments, 16-22 Coppergate; 4-8, 16: glass beads, 6-8 Pavement; 9-10: glass rings, 6-8 Pavement; 11: glass bead with gold foil covering, 16-22 Coppergate; 12-15 amber beads, 6-8 Pavement. Scale 1:1*

From Clifford Street came a large collection of unworked fragments of amber as well as a number of beads, divided by Waterman (1959, 95-6) into two groups: Type 1—tapering pendant beads of sub-rectangular cross-section; Type 2—cylindrical or disc-shaped beads of varying cross-section. Beads of Type 2 can clearly be seen from their regular outlines to have been lathe-turned. Many beads apparently had been broken in the course of perforation and the same fate has befallen a jet bead from 6-8 Pavement (Fig 23, 1): perhaps in preparation for finishing on a lathe, the block of jet had been roughly cut or chipped into shape, the central perforation having been started from either side. A broken jet ring was found during earlier excavations at Pavement (Waterman 1959, 104, Fig 25, 23).

Waterman (1959, 94, Fig 21, 3) illustrates a pendant of jet in the form of a coiled serpent, for which he cites several Scandinavian parallels. This piece is distinguished from all other jet objects of this period found in York by its realistic three-dimensional treatment and speaks of a

much more competent level of workmanship than can otherwise be discerned. Although found on the Railway Station site, which produced many Roman burials, this piece is generally agreed to be of Viking date (RCHMY 1, 143). Two playing-pieces of jet, one from Nessgate and the other found at Union Terrace (*Interim* 1, no 1, 29) may belong to the period of Scandinavian supremacy but are, perhaps, more likely to be of early post-Conquest date. Both are ornamented with incised ring-and-dot decoration, a motif which appears on two new discoveries from 11th or 12th century contexts at 16-22 Coppergate: each of these—a small pendant cross with a suspension hole in one of its equally-sized expanding arms (Fig 23, 3) and a large, flat pendant or bead, possibly broken during perforation (Fig 23, 2)—has the decoration enhanced by the inlaying of silver within the engraved ornament, a technique which seems otherwise to have been noted only at Winchester where two dice, both apparently residual, were similarly embellished with tin.[5]

Glass

Evidence of workshops producing glass beads has been found over the years in several vicinities, notably at Clifford Street and 7-13 Pavement. Those found at Clifford Street (Waterman 1959, 96; Radley 1971, 49) include many spoiled, misshapen, and broken beads, clearly the waste from a workshop in the immediate vicinity, while the heavy concentration (over 230 examples) from 7-13 Pavement has similar implications (Waterman 1959, 104; Radley 1971, 49-50). A cache of beads and waste fragments found more recently at 34 Shambles (Palliser & Hall 1975, 33), although very similar in appearance to those mentioned above, is almost certainly of 12th or early 13th century date; the possibility that the Clifford Street and 7-13 Pavement excavations may also have produced material of this late date cannot be ruled out.

The York beads include annular, cylindrical, biconical, segmented, and lobed or melon types in a variety of colours including orange, yellow, brown, green, blue, black, and white and they range in opacity from translucent to opaque. Occasionally colours are combined, threads of glass being trailed over a body of contrasting colour and, sometimes, marvered flush. A sheet of gold foil has been incorporated into a bead found at Clifford Street (Waterman 1959, 96, Fig 22, 33) and the same technique is found on two cylindrical beads with chamfered edges from the current excavations at 16-22 Coppergate (Fig 23, 11). A number of large annular or ring-shaped beads found in 1951 at 7-13 Pavement and more recently at 6-8 Pavement (Fig 23, 9-10) in yellow, green, and black glass may indeed be finger-rings (or, perhaps, hair ornaments) rather than necklace beads, while some cylindrical beads, usually in green glass (Fig 23, 4-8), are so small that they could perhaps have been sewn on to clothing to form decorative patterns or worn in a festoon to make a more striking visual impact.

Apart from these beads, objects of glass are rare in Anglo-Scandinavian York and their manufacture within the city cannot satisfactorily be demonstrated. They are limited to a few fragments of linen-smoother from Clifford Street (Waterman 1959, 96), 1 Parliament Street (Radley 1971, 50), and 6-8 Pavement (Fig 36, 4) and to a single rim fragment from a glass vessel found at Clifford Street. Although the possibility that this vessel could date from before the Scandinavian conquest has been raised in the past (Cramp 1967, 17-18), an origin as late as the 10th century remains a possibility (Waterman 1959, 96).

Metals

Blacksmiths and coppersmiths (and, to a lesser extent, silver and goldsmiths) must have formed an extremely important element among the craftsmen of Anglo-Scandinavian York, and yet primary evidence of their activities is very scarce indeed. Radley (1971, 48-9) was able to summarize all earlier finds in two short paragraphs: traces of iron-working in the form of slag were found at Feasegate (where it was possibly indicative of smelting) (Stead 1958, 537), Pavement, and Goodramgate (Radley 1971, 49), while a piece of vitrified furnace lining and traces of what was thought to be haematite were recovered from 1 Parliament Street (Radley 1971, 49). Two barrow-loads of thin copper sheets were found in High Ousegate by Benson (1902, 66) close to the remains of two 'furnaces', but no further details of these survive. The stone ring-mould from Hungate mentioned by Radley (1971, 49)

seems to be of medieval rather than Anglo-Scandinavian date (Richardson 1959, 100, Fig 28, 10) but a unique mould (Fig 24, 8) found more recently is undoubtedly of Anglo-Scandinavian origin; it was recovered from the bottom of a pit dug into Roman levels at 9 Blake Street, in the heart of the former Roman fortress. The mould fragment, of white, hard-fired clay, bears an impression of a trefoil brooch, a type which occurs fairly commonly in Scandinavia in bronze and also in precious metals (Petersen 1928, 93-114). The Anglo-Scandinavian style of ornament on this example clearly indicates that the type was not only adopted in England but that its development was further pursued here. Crucible fragments associated with the mould from Blake Street revealed traces of zinc, with the implication that either trefoil brooches were being produced in zinc bronze on this particular site or, perhaps more probably, that the rubbish pit served a workshop producing a range of goods in a variety of base and more noble metals. Evidently there was scope for the production of a single type of ornament in a variety of materials: a finger-ring of plaited gold wire (Fig 24, 10) found at Hungate, for example, finds more mundane counterparts in lead alloy from Bishophill (Fig 24, 11) and from 6-8 Pavement (Fig 24, 12). A second gold ring (Fig 24, 9) showing two confronted animals clasping a human head between their paws came from Fishergate: Cramp (1967, 18) has suggested a late 9th or early 10th century date for this piece and has postulated a possible connection with the cult of St Edmund, which had many adherents among the Scandinavian settlers. A lead-alloy figurine, possibly of early medieval date, from 6-8 Pavement (Fig 25), may have been connected with the same cult: the figurine represents a man with one arm outstretched and the other drawn back, as though he were an archer about to release an arrow. Leaden figures of this sort are usually fragments of the cheap souvenirs and devotional trinkets that were sold in vast numbers at important centres of medieval pilgrimage. Within this field of pilgrim souvenirs, the only comparable figure, according to information received from Brian Spencer, is that of an archer on a 14th century badge found near Hailes Abbey, Gloucestershire, depicting the martyrdom of St Edmund.

Other high-quality pieces of metalwork found (but not necessarily manufactured) in York include a scabbard chape with openwork ornament in Jellinge style (Waterman 1959, 72) found in Coppergate, a 10th century strap-end with Borre style interlace decoration (Fig 24, 2) from St Mary Bishophill Senior (Wilson 1965, 154-6), and a ring terminal (Fig 24, 4) found at Skeldergate, again from a strap or belt and decorated with relief ornament including what appear to be two addorsed birds. A heavy bronze armlet with punched decoration (Fig 24, 1) is also of this period; similar punching appears on the head of a small loose ring-headed pin from 36 St Andrewgate (Fig 28, 5) which may be compared with another example from Birka (Arbman 1943, Abb 218, 43).

To the four disc brooches already known from York (Waterman 1959, 79, Fig 10, 7-9; Richardson 1959, 81, Fig 18, 2), excavations by the Trust have added another three examples: two of these come from 16-22 Coppergate and are, respectively, a domed brooch of lead alloy with openwork decoration in the Borre style (Fig 24, 5) and a flat discoid brooch with a low relief design of spiralling tendrils on the surface, perhaps imitating filigree, and with a pivot and catch-plate on the rear (Fig 24, 6); the third example, found in 1973 at Bishophill, has a central boss ornamented with a petal-like design on a hatched background, surrounded by alternating panels of chevrons and dots (Fig 24, 7).

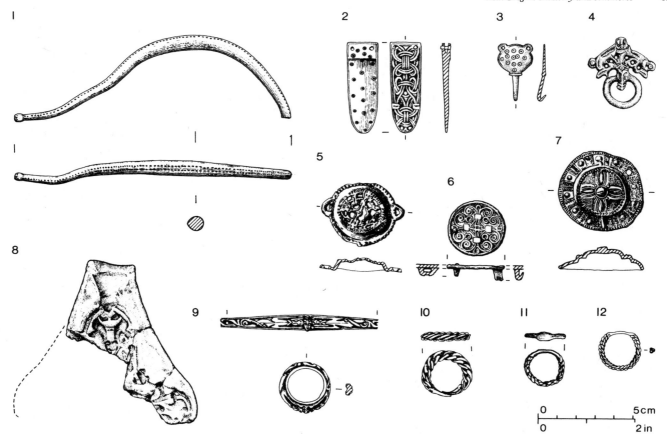

Fig 24   *Ornamental metalwork: 1: bronze armlet, 21-3 Aldwark; 2: bronze strap-end, St Mary Bishophill Senior; 3: bronze hooked fastener, 6-8 Pavement; 4: bronze strap-end with ring terminal, Skeldergate; 5-6: pewter brooches, 16-22 Coppergate; 7: pewter brooch, Bishophill; 8: clay mould for trefoil brooch, 9 Blake Street; 9: gold ring, Fishergate; 10: gold ring, Hungate; 11: pewter ring, Bishophill; 12: pewter ring, 6-8 Pavement. Scale 1:2*

One or two bone 'trial pieces' found in York may conceivably have been used for impressing clay moulds from which decorative plates of bronze or precious metal could have been cast. Objects of this sort are illustrated by Grove (1940, 285-7) and Waterman (1959, 91, Pl XX, 1); since neither of them is very highly finished, however, they are probably no more than practice pieces.

The production of fine metalwork must at all times have been secondary to that of iron tools, implements, and weapons. Waterman (1959, 71) commented on the paucity of weapons of Viking type found in York and since that time no new finds have been made. The numerous knives which have been found (Fig 26, 1-2) belong in the category of tools rather than weapons and may be grouped with the awls (Fig 26, 3-6) of which several were found at the leatherworking site at 6-8 Pavement (see below) and with a fairly numerous group of implements with elongated spoon-shaped ends (Fig 26, 7-8). The occurrence of one of these implements in the same context as the wood-turning debris from Coppergate described below (p 51) seems to raise the possibility that some of these may be wood-turners' gouges, but the more orthodox identification given to them is that they are drill bits; the occurrence

Fig 25   *Lead alloy figurine, 6-8 Pavement. Scale 1:1*

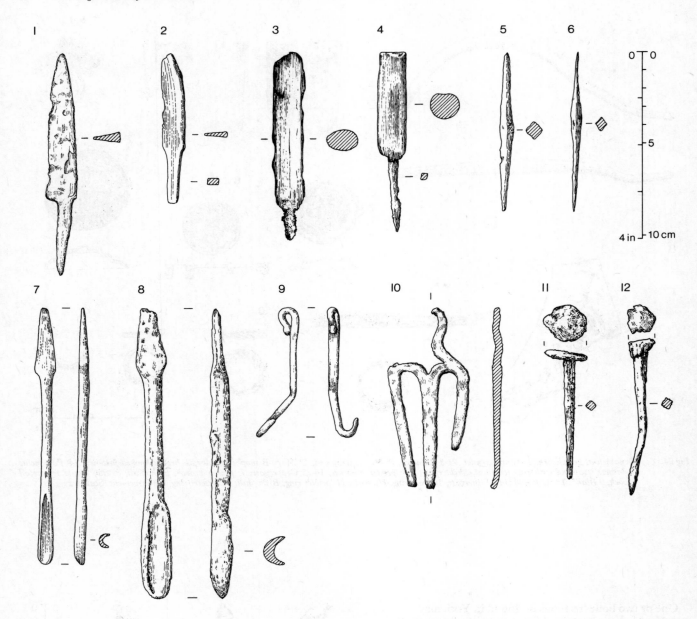

Fig 26   Iron implements etc: 1: knife, 6-8 Pavement; 2: knife, Skeldergate; 3-6: awls (3 and 4 with wooden handles), 6-8 Pavement; 7: spoon-bit or reamer, 16-22 Coppergate; 8: spoon-bit or reamer, 21-3 Aldwark; 9-12: miscellaneous ironwork, 6-8 Pavement. Scale 1:2

at Mileham, Norfolk, of one of these tools complete with a transverse handle (Wilson 1968a, 146-7; 1976c, 258) certainly favours the latter identification, and the flattened tang with which implements of this sort are usually provided is appropriate to withstand the torsion associated with a drill. However, differences in detail may allow for more than one specialized function: the closed ends on some of these tools from Anglo-Scandinavian contexts (Fig 26, 7-8) seem to have no cutting value whatever, which might rule them out as drills, although the flattened tangs would suit transverse handles; the suggestion [6] that some at least may be reamers rather than spoon bits seems to reconcile all these considerations. Detailed study of the large numbers of these implements found throughout the country in Anglo-Scandinavian and early medieval contexts would certainly repay the effort involved.

A number of woodman's and carpenter's axes from the city have been noted by Waterman (1959, 72, Fig 5, 5-7). Three further examples from York of broadly contemporary date are in the Sheffield City Museum's Bateman Collection (Howarth 1899, 239). Other ironwork of this period includes various items of horse furniture (Waterman 1959, 74-6), and various locks and keys (Fig 27). A small mortice lock from 6-8 Pavement (Fig 27, 1) survived almost intact: inside a hollowed-out housing of oak lay a spindle over which the hollow stem of the key had fitted, a mortice bolt with a notch in which the bit engaged, and a retaining spring to keep the bolt in position. Two bolts from similar locks came from the same site (Fig 27, 4-5). A padlock of more complex construction was found at Hungate (Richardson 1959, 81, Fig 18, 4) and more recently another example (Fig 27, 2) has come from Skeldergate: the casing is of sheet iron, ornamented with zig-zag wire decoration; copper corrosion products around the edges of the casing and the wire suggest that the entire assembly was brazed. The loop or shackle slides within an external tubular housing. Little can now be distinguished of the inner workings, but from the form of the keyhole it appears that the mechanism was operated by a conventional twist key; a similar arrangement can be seen on padlocks from Birka (Arbman 1943, 420, Taf 273, 6) and Helgö (Holmqvist & Arrhenius 1964, Fig 19; Holmqvist 1961, Pl 34; 1970, Fig 13), while the more common barrel-lock system with a sliding key was evidently used on the Hungate lock, which has a T-shaped key slot of the type present in a number of the Birka locks (Arbman 1943, Taf 273, 1-2, 4-5) and on other examples from Trelleborg (Nørlund 1948, Tav XXIV, 1-2) and Helgö (Holmqvist & Arrhenius 1964, Fig 20). A number of slide (Fig 27, 3) and twist (Fig 27, 6-7) keys have also been found.

Articles of this degree of complexity (cf also the balances in Fig 28, 4, 7) show a very high level of technological sophistication among contemporary metalworkers. Not only were they capable of forging intricate components to a fairly high degree of accuracy but they were also familiar with the techniques of soldering (as displayed by the padlocks) and metal plating; this may be seen from the sheet bronze applied to certain iron stirrups (Waterman 1959, 76) and the more accomplished tinning seen on a bronze mount with zoomorphic head from 6-8 Pavement (Fig 28, 1) and on the iron ring-headed pin from All Saints, Pavement (Fig 28, 3). The technique seems, therefore, to have been more widely used than has hitherto been thought (cf Jope 1956, 35-42). When judged by this level of craftsmanship and by the fluent decorative schemes with which they ornamented their finer work, it is clear that the metalworkers of York had little to learn from their contemporaries anywhere else in northern Europe.

Stone

The craft of the stonemason was one which enjoyed a considerable expansion in the York area during the Anglo-Scandinavian period. Elsewhere (pp 11-20), J T Lang equates the burgeoning of a number of local sculptural schools with the increasing prosperity of York and notes a new secular emphasis in their output which, for the most part, takes the form of funerary sculpture. That York lay at the commercial as well as the artistic centre of this new movement cannot be doubted: the patronage of the wealthy merchant class quickly outstripped that of religious institutions and led to a greatly expanded market in carved

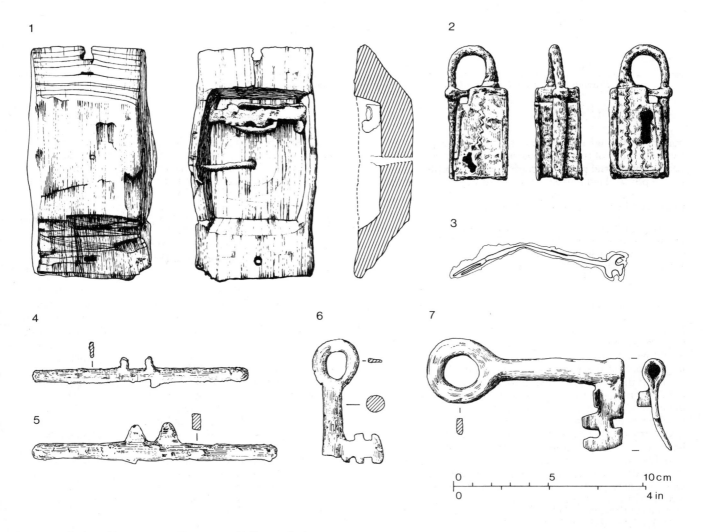

Fig 27   Locks and keys: 1, 3-7: 6-8 Pavement; 2: Skeldergate. Scale 1:2

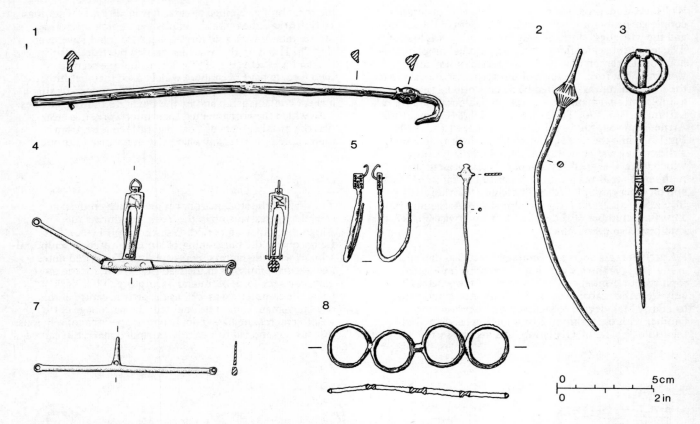

Fig 28   Bronze and ironwork: 1: tinned bronze mount with zoomorphic terminal, 6-8 Pavement; 2: bronze pin with applied collar, 6-8 Pavement; 3: tinned iron pin, All Saints Pavement; 4, 7: bronze balances, 9 Blake Street; 5, 6: pins, 36 St Andrewgate; 8: adjoining rings, 6-8 Pavement. Scale 1:2

masonry. We may look forward to the discovery one day of the workshops of these masons; among the broken debris and tentative trial pieces discarded by the sculptors may lie the physical evidence for the evolution of many of the artistic traits whose development is only imperfectly understood from the surviving monuments.

Little work has been carried out on the identification of the quarry sources which fed this industry, but it is clear that some use was made of pre-existing Roman masonry (Pattison 1973, 211-3).

Bone and antler

Evidence of bone and antler working has been recovered from many of the major sites excavated within the Anglo-Scandinavian city, testifying to a greater economic importance for these raw materials than has hitherto been accorded them. In particular, antler—almost exclusively red deer antler—rather than skeletal bone was clearly a material of considerable commercial value. Wherever the basal burrs of these antlers are found, they very frequently display natural ruptures, indicating that they have been shed in the annual moult; antlers derived from slaughtered beasts occur less often, according more closely with the comparatively infrequent occurrence of deer bones among contemporary food refuse from the city (p 63). Similar situations have been noted in contemporary Dublin (Ó Ríordáin 1971, 75), Århus (Andersen *et al* 1971, 121), Hedeby (Reichstein 1969, 63 ff), and in early medieval Lund (Bergquist & Lepiksaar (1957, 21). Since most

red deer shed their antlers within a fairly limited period of time (around May of each year), we may suppose that some very intensive collecting activity went on in the surrounding forests in order to provide for this city-based industry, which was surely in professional hands and therefore demanded a year-round supply of raw materials. Bone was occasionally utilized in the manufacture of items such as combs (see below, Fig 29, 10) but its use seems generally to have been scorned in favour of antler except in the production of dress pins (Fig 30) and other small items (Fig 31, 6-12).

An interesting piece of place-name evidence may be brought to notice here: Hartergate, one of York's former street names with the Scandinavian 'gate' ending, has been derived (Smith, A H, 1937, 289) from the Old Scandinavian personal name *Hjǫrtr* (genitive *Hjartar*), implying that it took its name from some historical personage, perhaps a resident. However, precisely the same term was used to denote a hart or deer (cf Cleasby *et al* 1962, 266, 268): considering the amount of debris from antler-working which has been found in the vicinity of the former Hartergate (now Friargate, leading from Clifford Street to Castlegate), a derivation from the 'hartshorners' who carried on their trade in the area would seem equally attractive. Although the medieval horners (who worked principally with cattle horn rather than antler) have given their name to streets in many cities (cf Hornpot Lane in York), a correlation with the antler workers, whose trade seems to have declined (probably in favour of the horners to a large extent) from about the 12th or 13th century, does not seem previously to have been postulated.[7]

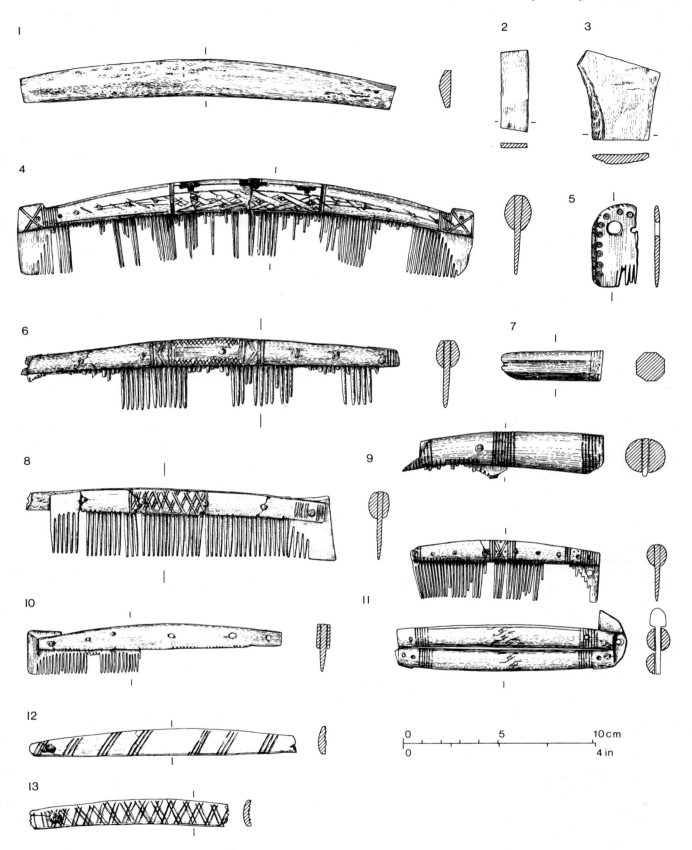

Fig 29 Bone and antler combs: 1: prepared antler blank, 5 Coppergate; 2-3: prepared antler blanks, 6-8 Pavement; 4: antler comb with decorative perforations, Clifford Street; 5: comb fragment of Frisian type, 6-8 Pavement; 6: antler comb, Coppergate; 7, 9: antler comb handles, Skeldergate; 8: antler comb, 21-3 Aldwark; 10: antler comb with split rib side-plates, Clifford Street; 11: antler comb and case, 16-22 Coppergate; 12-13: split-rib comb case fragments, Leadmill Lane. Scale 1:2

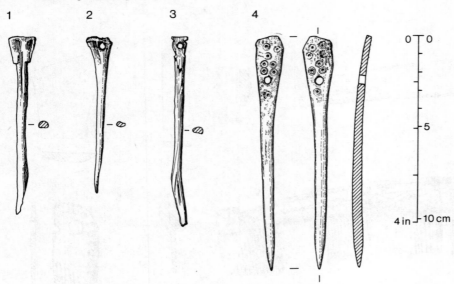

Fig 30   *Bone pins: 1-3: 6-8 Pavement; 4: Skeldergate. Scale 1:2*

A variety of bone and antler objects is described by Waterman (1959, 80-93), of which the most numerous are utilized tines. But while quite a large proportion of the tines from any one site may have been put to good use (Fig 31, 1-5) they were almost always of secondary importance, representing (along with the many sawn burrs) merely the waste from trimming the main beam. In the manufacture of mounts and of combs (over 95% of which are made of antler), the standard procedure was for the burr and the tines to be sawn off and the remaining beam to be sawn into appropriate lengths; these were then cut lengthwise into strips of the desired width and the cancellous inner tissue removed, leaving a flat rectangular strip which could be cut or filed into its final shape. In the manufacture of combs, two elements were involved— the thin and flat tooth plates (Fig 29, 2-3) and the more robust connecting plates or crossbars (Fig 29, 1) between which the tooth plates were riveted before the teeth were cut with a fine saw. An interesting exception to this general rule is a comb from Clifford Street which has side plates made from split ribs; their slender, flat cross-sections (Fig 29, 10) immediately distinguish them from their more bulky antler counterparts (Fig 29, 4, 6, 8). Split ribs were also used in the manufacture of a number of comb cases (Fig 29, 12-13), fragments of which were found with other debris in a rubbish pit in Leadmill Lane. With around one hundred combs of Anglo-Scandinavian type now recovered from York as well as a considerable amount of manufacturing debris, they can truly be said to have represented a major industry which, to judge from the high quality of most of them[8], was certainly in the hands of professional craftsmen.

A number of antler points with incised decoration (Hall 1976a, Fig 14; Howarth 1899, 226) demonstrate that the bone and antler workers of the city were capable of some artistic virtuosity as well as technical excellence. One styliform pin from Clifford Street has an attractive dragonesque head (Waterman 1959, 82-3, Fig 12, 6), but while there are a few others of some artistic merit (*ibid*, Fig 12, 10-11) the majority are quite commonplace and may well have been carved from food bones by the individual

as required. Apart from the items mentioned above, bone and antler were used in the manufacture of knife-handles (Waterman 1959, Fig 7, 8-12), buckles, ornaments, playing pieces, and other small objects (*ibid*, Fig 19). Bone skates are quite common finds (Fig 31, 11), most of them fashioned from the metapodials of horses and cattle (MacGregor 1976, 57-74) and probably made by the individual as required. The presence of ivory fragments, on the other hand, apparently wasters from the manufacture of ornaments (p 39), hints at a professionally organized luxury trade employing imported ivory.

A range of well-developed implements must have been used in this industry: among these may be counted saws (including some very fine ones used with great skill in cutting comb teeth), axes, adzes, and draw-knives for getting the material roughly into shape, and files or other abrasive tools for finishing it off; a variety of drills from *c* 3mm to *c* 15mm are attested by rivet and suspension holes, while a range of scribers or centre-bits would have been needed for producing the ubiquitous ring-and-dot decoration. Knives would presumably have been used to produce zoomorphic and low-relief interlace (Fig 29, 4). Occasionally, other materials such as gilt bronze sheet were combined with bone and antler to provide an ornamental backing, as in the case of a casket from Coppergate (Waterman 1959, 86-7) and a comb (Fig 29, 4), with T-shaped openings on the side plates; this technique is found on a number of contemporary combs from Scandinavia (Blomqvist 1942, 142 ff; Long 1975, 27, Fig 9, 6) and on two others from England (Smith, R A, 1902, 233, Fig 16; 1909, 164-5, Fig 27).

Wood

Large quantities of timber must have been consumed by the Anglo-Scandinavian city for a variety of purposes, ranging from the reinforcement of the defensive ramparts and the construction of timber-framed and plank-built houses to the manufacture of small objects of everyday use. An appropriate range of craftsmen, each with some degree

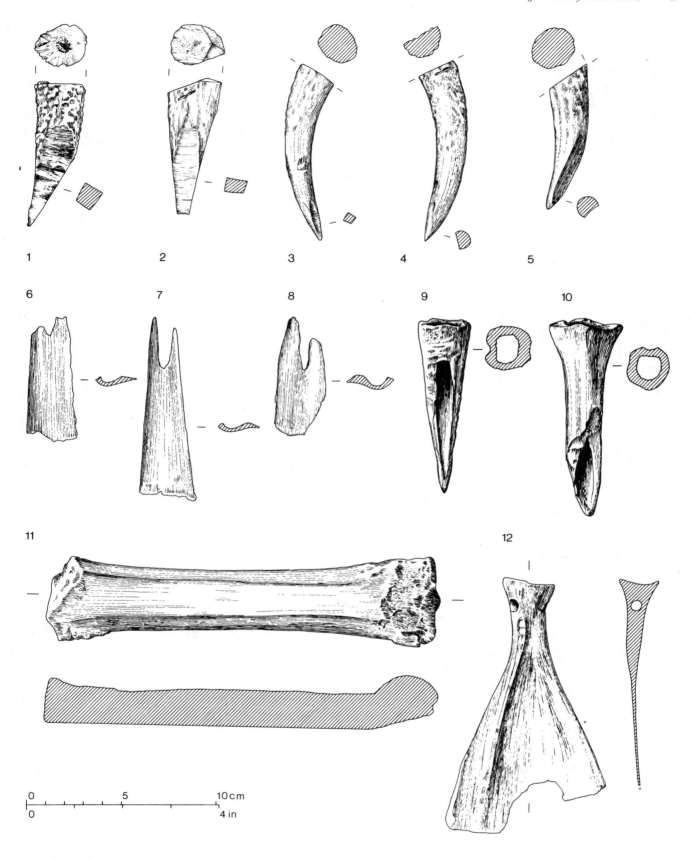

Fig 31   Bone and antler implements: 1-5: utilized antler tines, 5 Coppergate; 6-8: utilized cattle nasal bones, 6-8 Pavement; 9-10: socketed bone points, 6-8 Pavement; 11: bone skate, Leadmill Lane; 12: scapula scoop, 6-8 Pavement. Scale 1:2

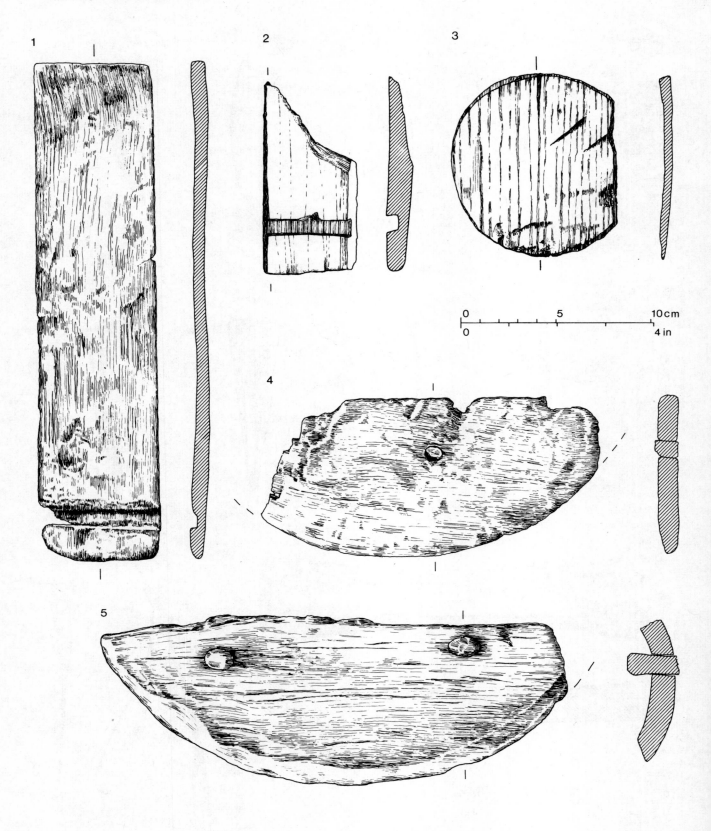

Fig 32   Stave-built vessels: 1-2: staves, 6-8 Pavement; 3-5: bases or heads, 6-8 Pavement. Scale 1:2

of specialization, must be postulated. Among those not involved in construction work, two groups may be singled out for special notice—those producing barrels and casks and other stave-built containers and those who specialized in lathe turning.

Products of the turners or coopers who gave their name to Coppergate (Smith, A H, (1937, 285) derives it from Old Scandinavian *Koppari*—a joiner or turner) have been unearthed from several sites. At 6-8 Pavement the remains of large discs of oak (Fig 32, 4-5) up to 0.32m in diameter were recovered from the building contractor's spoil, and it seems certain that these represent the ends of stave-built casks. An oak disc of 0.25m diameter from Hungate has been similarly identified (Richardson 1959, 86). A disc of only 100mm diameter from 6-8 Pavement (Fig 32, 3) may have come from a much smaller vessel, corresponding to the stave-built mugs postulated by Hencken (1950, 154) at Lagore Crannog, Co Meath, while two parallel-sided staves from the same site (Fig 32, 1-2) are probably from buckets. Each of the latter staves has an internal channel 10mm wide into which the base would have fitted, while one of them bears on its external face, which is otherwise badly charred, the outline of a hoop in the form of a band of sound wood some 15mm wide, protected from the fire by the now missing hoop. On analogy with the 9th century stave-built containers from Lissue Rath, Co Antrim (Bersu 1947, 53), either iron or wooden hoops could have been used. Both staves have been cut with a saw and one shows signs of having been dressed on its outer surface with an adze.

Lathe-turned vessels have been recovered more frequently than their stave-built counterparts. All those so far discovered have been bowls of open form, but the occurrence of a flanged lid fragment (Fig 33, 2) at 6-8 Pavement suggests that the range of products produced by the York wood-turners was somewhat more varied. A fragment from a small bowl or cup from the same site (Fig 33, 4), with its outer surface incised with a basketwork pattern, has similar implications. Of the bowls from this site, one proved to be made of oak (*Quercus* sp) and four were of unidentified softwoods; one base fragment (Fig 33, 5) has been identified as field maple (*Acer campestre*), thought to be the species from which three bowls recovered from King's Square (Wenham 1968, 167, Fig 3) and one from Hungate (Richardson 1959, 86, Fig 20) were made. A wooden bowl of unknown species was also found at 1 Parliament Street (Radley 1971, 52, Fig 11, 14). Bowls of this sort were evidently prized; the Hungate bowl, for example, was considered worthwhile repairing with iron staples after it had split.

Current excavations at 16-22 Coppergate have produced valuable evidence to complement these bowls. Eight cores (Fig 33, 7-9), all of them of ash (*Fraxinus excelsior*), were found along with masses of wood shavings and undoubtedly represent the debris from a wood-turning shop. Similar finds have been made during excavations at Hedeby (Schietzel 1970, 80-1, Abb 3) and at Lissue Rath (Bersu 1947, 54, Fig 14, 4-5). Our knowledge of lathes of the Viking period is, of course, entirely inferential, but it seems likely that they would not have differed greatly from the foot-operated pole lathe, with a large return spring in the form of a bough, which appears illustrated in a 13th century manuscript in the Bibliothèque Nationale, Paris (MS lat 11560, f.84(1), reproduced in Salzman 1964, 172).[9]

A number of small items of wood, although not amounting to evidence for an 'industry', serve to demonstrate the range of products in this medium: among these may be included the box or casket from Coppergate already mentioned, two wooden spoons from Clifford Street (Waterman 1959, 86) and a hawthorn or applewood flute from Hungate (Richardson 1959, 85).

Leather

As the principal market town of Northumbria, York would have been assured of a constant influx of livestock on the hoof. Butchering was carried out in the heart of the city, centering by an early date on the Shambles (*Flesshamelles*—flesh-shambles or flesh-benches—perhaps ultimately of Old English origin) first recorded in Domesday Book. An important by-product of this meat trade lay in the hides from slaughtered animals, which formed the raw material for a flourishing leather industry. Several distinct skills are involved in the preparation of hides and the manufacture and repair of leather goods. A number of these were recognized by the creation of distinct guilds quite early in the medieval period. Radley (1971, 51) has noted that by 1278 the following trades were represented among the freemen of York: skinner, tanner, dresser, glover, girdler, harness-maker, parchment-maker, and cobbler. To what extent these craft distinctions had already emerged in Anglo-Scandinavian England is impossible to say, although cobblers' shops have been postulated on the evidence from offcuts at two sites—Feasegate (Dyer & Wenham 1958, 422) and Hungate (Richardson 1959, 63-4), the latter excavation producing, in addition to many small offcuts, a number of old shoe uppers with pieces cut out of them as though for patching (cf Ó Ríordáin 1971, 75). Some distinct skills within the leatherworking trade may, therefore, already have become identifiable.

The process of tanning is best represented in the city by the series of pits unearthed during the winter of 1902-3 at 25-7 High Ousegate, interpreted as the remains of a tannery (Benson 1902, 64-7). Of three large pits, each some 7m × 3m and set end to end, that on the High Ousegate frontage had 0.30m of puddled clay at the bottom, the next in line contained some 0.23m of yellow sand, and the third had 0.13m of lime. From the traces of sill beams associated with the pits, Radley (1971, 43, Fig 10) surmised that the tannery was housed in a building some 27.5m long and 5m wide, with galleries or aisles just over 1m in width on either side. A number of internal divisions were marked by cross beams, several of which passed over the tan pits and, it was suggested, may have formed part of a series of racks on which the skins were hung at various stages in the process, while a series of adjacent drainage channels may have serviced the whole complex. The clay and sand found in two of the pits may simply represent accumulated silting from the washing of hides (although the clear distinction between the two kinds of sediment seems to imply different detailed procedures), while the lime evidently derives from the slaking process used in de-hairing the skins. The presence of abundant limestone fragments at 1 Parliament Street and 2-4 Pavement has been thought (Radley 1971, 51) to derive from the same process. Further excavations at 6-8 Pavement by York Archaeological Trust produced evidence which may indicate alternative de-hairing techniques: it has been suggested (Buckland *et al* 1974, 29) that the numerous elder seeds (*Sambucus nigra*) from the site may have been used in an acid ferment for de-hairing hides while patches of wood ash or charcoal could have been used in solution either for de-hairing and de-fatting skins (as described in Ryder 1963, 541) or to make them more supple (cf Reed 1972, 165). Feathers and eggshell fragments from associated layers may have derived from chicken dung brought in for the same purposes.

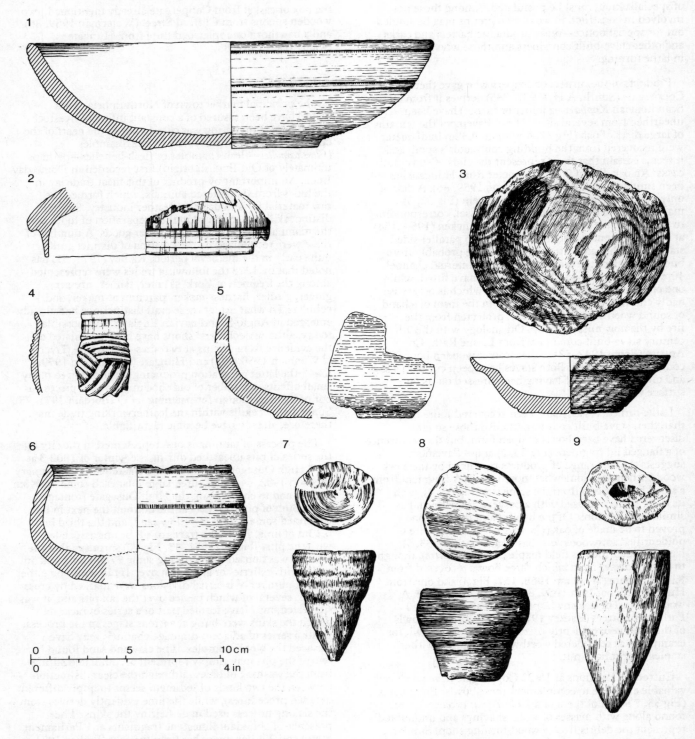

Fig 33   Lathe-turned bowls etc: 1, 4-6: bowls and cups, 6-8 Pavement; 2: flanged lid, 6-8 Pavement; 3: bowl, 16-22 Coppergate; 7-9: turned cores from wooden bowls, 16-22 Coppergate. Scale 1:2

Wherever the agent could be identified (Richardson 1959, 90; Radley 1971, 50) the leather fragments from York have all been found to be tanned with vegetable tannins. Indeed, until the mid 19th century, 90% of English leather was bark tanned (Clarkson 1974, 136-52). Salzman (1964, 247-8) records that the inventories of six tanners operating in Colchester *c* 1300 all include quantities of oak bark and mentions the prohibition of the use of

bark other than oak. Berkergate in York is thought (Smith, A H, 1937, 300) to have received its name from the tanneries it once housed. Although no evidence for alum tawing (the principal alternative to bark tanning) has yet been found in York, Radley (1971, 51) notes that the presence of jet workshops in the city implies that there were links with the area around Whitby, where alum occurs naturally and in quantity.

When the hides had been immersed for a sufficient time in the tanning solution they would have been stretched out to dry on frames: several offcuts from 6-8 Pavement are pierced by holes distorted by strain, probably resulting from prolonged lashing on a frame. In the interests of space saving, hides would probably have been stretched in this way on vertical frames, although some settings of stakes driven into the floors and wall footings at 6-8 Pavement have also been interpreted as possible stretchers (Addyman 1975a, 221, Pl XLI, c).

Most of the leather so far recovered from Anglo-Scandinavian levels is from adult cattle skins, but calf hide has been noted from 2-4 Pavement (Radley 1971, 51) and (perhaps) deer skin from Hungate (Richardson 1959, 90).

As to finished goods, the majority of leather finds from the city are shoes or ankle boots, with good collections coming from Feasegate (Dyer & Wenham 1958, 422-3; Thornton & Goodfellow, in Stead 1958, 525-30), Hungate (Richardson 1959, 86-90) and, more recently, from 6-8 Pavement and 5 Coppergate (MacGregor, forthcoming). Typical shoes are made on the turnshoe principle with whole-cut (one piece) uppers, side-seamed at the instep and blind-stitched to a single-thickness sole. Some have triangular reinforcings at the heel (Richardson 1959, 89). Fastenings are generally absent from these shoes, which were simply slipped over the feet. Ankle boots too generally have whole-cut uppers with instep seams, but also incorporate a flap which was fastened over the instep with a toggle and loop arrangement (Fig 34, 1). The toggle was made by cutting an elongated T-shaped strip, slitting the transverse piece and threading the stem tightly through it, so forming a rigid roll; the loop with which it engaged was cut from a second strip of leather, split at the lower end, the free ends being passed through perforations in the side of the boot and tied together on the inside. The same method of forming leather toggles survived, at least on the continent, into the late medieval period (Groenman-van Waateringe & Velt 1975, 110, Abb 12). The sole was blind-stitched to the upper in the same manner as with the shoes, except that the heel arrangement was more complex: instead of the sole following the outline of the foot at the heel, it was extended to a point (cf Fig 34, 3) which fitted with a closed seam into a V-shaped cut in the rear quarters of the upper. Occasional instances of shoes being soled in this way are also found (Thornton & Goodfellow, in Stead 1958, 529, Fig 6, 4). The stitching medium used in the manufacture of these shoes was usually animal fibre (perhaps wool) or leather thonging (Fig 34, 4); one shoe from Feasegate, however, was sewn with bast thread, probably flax (Dyer & Wenham 1958, 422-3, Fig 3). Stitching around the top of the upper was noted on the latter shoe and also occurred on examples from Hungate (Richardson 1959, 90) and 5 Coppergate (Fig 34, 1). Richardson (1959) suggests that this stitching may have secured a lining but, alternatively, it may indicate the use of edge bindings as on the important series of shoes from Lund (Blomqvist 1938, 216), over 90% of which have stitch holes around the ankle opening.

Further connections may be noted with contemporary shoes from northern Europe: Hald (1972, 150-1) has already suggested that boots with instep flaps as described above equate with those found, for example, at Walcheren, in Zeeland, Holland, in the ship-burial at Oseberg, Norway, and in the Scandinavian emporium of Staraja Ladoga in Russia. These northern European connections are strengthened by the occurrence of soles with pointed heels at Middelburg (Walcheren), Schleswig, Oseberg, and Lund, as well as Staraja Ladoga and Novgorod, with dates ranging from the 7th to the 14th centuries. While the type may have been brought to this country with other Scandinavian traits in the 9th and 10th centuries, its occurrence in earlier Frisian contexts on the continent allows for an alternative pre-Norse introduction.

Several leather scabbards have been recovered from York, most of them plain and seamed up the centre of one of the broad faces. They vary in length from c 0.20m at Hungate (Richardson 1959, 86, Fig 19, 25) to over 0.50m at 6-8 Pavement, indicating a variety of implements and weapons ranging from knives to short swords. A recent and more impressive find is the knife scabbard illustrated in Fig 35, 1, recovered from the spoil from a mechanically-excavated sewer trench in Parliament Street.[10] It measures 0.35m in length and has rivet holes along one edge. Although now slightly damaged, the throat bears signs of having been protected originally by a guard; alternatively, the perforations and markings at the throat may derive from the attachment of a suspension loop, so that the scabbard could be slung below a belt in the fashion shown on several crosses from Middleton, North Yorkshire (Lang 1973, 17, Pl iv, 1-3). The second attachment point necessary for suspension in this way was evidently at the centre of the scabbard, where marked concentric scoring seems to indicate a point about which the scabbard swivelled; it may originally have been protected here by a plate. (The scabbards on the Middleton Crosses are thought (ibid), in contrast, to be supported by a second suspension loop at the tip.) The embossed ornament on both sides shows decoratively the form of the knife for which the scabbard was designed, consisting of a blade with angled back and a handle; a guard seems to be indicated on the front by a roundel containing a coiled beast and on the back by a plain rectangular field. The handle and the blade on the front are covered with irregular interlace and on the back with much looser and thinner strands interlacing in a more formal manner in a regular zig-zag. The area on the front not occupied by the representation of the knife is filled with hatched triangular fields. Only the pommel of the knife would have protruded from the sheath, so that its overall length was probably in the region of 0.38m. Two comparable, though fragmentary scabbards may be noted from Cheapside (*Antiq J*, **7** (1927), 526-7) and from nearby Lawrence Lane (*Antiq J*, **12** (1932), 177) in London (see also Russel 1939, 134-6).[11] Like these, the York scabbard is likely to date from the 10th or 11th century. A similar date may be proposed for a smaller scabbard (Fig 35, 2) from the same sewer trench: this example has been stitched rather than riveted and has a large sub-rectangular suspension hole. On the front, the handle and blade of the embossed knife design are filled with key and interlace decoration, the handle also having an interlace knot within a lozenge, while on the reverse, the blade is marked with tendrils and dots and the handle with a key pattern. A pommel can be distinguished at the top and the remainder of the surface is largely filled with rows of pellets. There is a curious and so far unexplained curving ridge moulded along the back of the blade on the principal face.

Most other leather finds from the city are fragments from straps and various indeterminate objects, but one important piece deserves mention here: the late Mr John Waterer has recently identified a large composite object from 6-8 Pavement as a shabrack, a piece of harness which would have fitted under a high wooden saddle, with various slots provided for girth and stirrup straps. A full account of this piece has been prepared by Mr Waterer for inclusion in MacGregor, forthcoming. Such a complex article, although so far unique in this period, serves to remind us

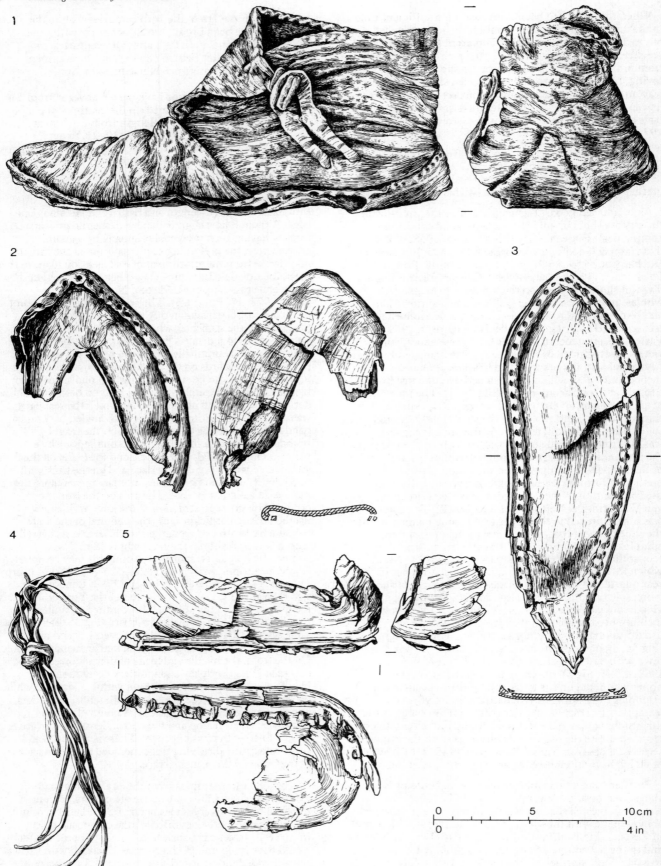

Fig 34   Boots and shoes: 1: ankle boot, 5 Coppergate; 2, 3, 5: shoe fragments, 6-8 Pavement; 4: thonging, 6-8 Pavement. Scale 1:2

1   2

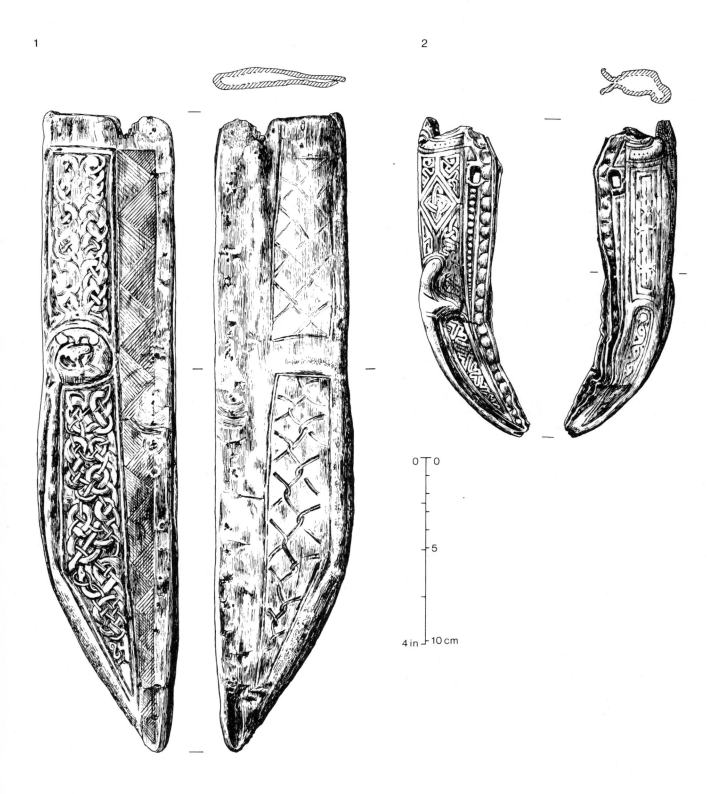

0⊤0

5

4 in⊥10 cm

Fig 35   Leather knife scabbards with embossed decoration, Parliament Street (sewer trench). Scale 1:2

that the repertoires of the leather craftsmen of Anglo-Scandinavian York were probably rarely as limited as the few chance survivals generally imply.

Textiles

Excavations at 6-8 Pavement produced a range of textile fragments in various weaves. Most were of wool and included diamond and chevron twills as well as examples in plain weave; there were also some plain woven linen fragments. These textiles are the subject of a major study by Mr John Hedges, which will appear in MacGregor, forthcoming. Several distinct groups have been identified by Mr Hedges (see Addyman 1975a, Pl XLIV) and these will no doubt form the basis of future research in this country, representing as they do by far the largest collection of Anglo-Scandinavian period textiles found to date in the British Isles.

Only one earlier find from York of broadly contemporary cloth has been noted: a single fragment of material in plain weave, Z-spun in one system and S-spun in the other, came from a 'Dark Ages' level at Feasegate (Stead 1958, 525).

None of these pieces need necessarily have been manufactured in York, however, but there is ample evidence to demonstrate that the city certainly did support a well-established textile industry: to what extent it was a cottage industry, carried on in any number of households, however, is still unclear. Spindle whorls in a variety of materials including stone (Fig 36, 1), chalk, jet, pottery, and bone (Fig 36, 2) have been found on several sites dating to the period under discussion, testifying to a considerable spinning activity, while annular loom weights of baked clay have been recovered from Castle Yard (Grove 1939, 113; O'Neil 1939, 89), Hungate (Richardson 1959, 85, Fig 19, 22), Clifford Street (Radley 1971, 52) and 6-8 Pavement (Fig 36, 3). Weights of this type imply that the looms in common use were of the vertical warp-weighted type. Mr Hedges' detailed examination of the weaving

patterns (and, in particular, of the occasional errors which they display) has thrown a great deal of new light on weaving practice in this period, including information on the knitting of the heddles, the use of Z- and S-spun threads, etc. Some possible traces of reddish dye have been noted on one of the Lloyds Bank fragments from 6-8 Pavement, although the evidence is not unequivocal. The presence on the same site of certain dye plants and of beetles sometimes associated with them (see p 63) may be significan in this context.

The implications of a single fragment of silk, found during excavations at 5 Coppergate, have already been discussed on p 40.

Pottery

No pottery of the Saxo-Norman series which, as its name implies, spans the period from the pre-Scandinavian phase until after the Norman conquest, has yet been shown to have been made in the city of York, so that what survives is evidently the result of commercial enterprise on the part of pottery-producing centres elsewhere which exploited the outlets provided by the York markets. With the exception of the three sherds of red-painted ware referred to above (p 39), all the pottery so far encountered is of English manufacture and is generally attributable to one or other of four major groups[12]:

York Ware   Hard ware with heavy tempering of angular quartz grits. Varies in colour from black through grey and buff to reddish brown. The type was first isolated by Stead (1958, 522) and was subsequently discussed by Le Patourel (1965, 109-10) and Hurst (1969a, 60). No kilns have yet been discovered, but preliminary mineral analyses suggest an origin in Yorkshire (though not in the immediate vicinity of York).

Torksey type ware   So named on account of its close resemblance to the kiln products of Torksey, Lincolnshire

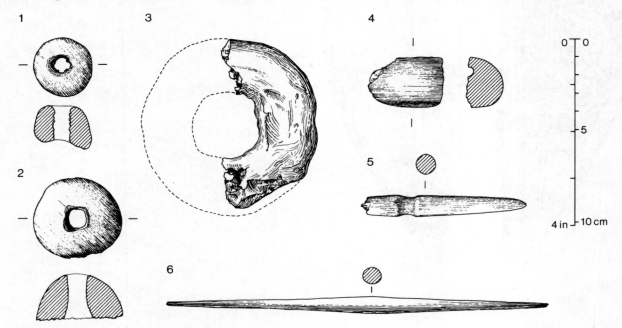

Fig 36   Spinning and weaving equipment: 1: stone whorl; 2: bone (femur head) whorl; 3: baked clay loom-weight; 4: glass linen smoother; 5: wooden bobbin or spindle; 6: bone pin-beater. All from 6-8 Pavement. Scale 1:2

(Barley 1964, 175-87). It is characterized by its sandy fabric, varying in colour from black to grey, buff, and brown.

St Neots type ware   Smooth grey or buff ware with crushed calcite temper. The majority of fragments in this fabric from York are less 'soapy' to the touch than true St Neots ware, which is generally tempered with shell rather than calcite. No kilns producing this fabric have yet been located.

Stamford type ware   Smooth grey to orange-buff wares, sometimes with yellow or sage-green glaze. The type is discussed by Hurst (1958, 37 ff).

The pottery described above can be shown to have reached York from a variety of sources more or less distant from the city. While the links with the Yorkshire hinterland implied by the occurrence of York type wares are no more than should be expected, contacts established with the potteries of Lincolnshire in the 10th century were apparently maintained for a period approaching two centuries and testify to a well-developed and stable pattern of commercial life such as cannot otherwise be apprehended archaeologically for the period.

Coinage

Elsewhere (pp 26-31), Professor Michael Dolley reviews the development of the Anglo-Scandinavian mint in York. After a generation or so in which even the copper *stycas* which had circulated before the Danish incursions disappeared, the first issues of a vigorous new silver coinage made their début. Subsequent issues not only mirror the political fortunes of the city but also reflect its continuing eminence as the major commercial centre of northern England. In their geographical distribution throughout the British Isles and, to some extent, on the Continent, no doubt there lie important clues from which further research will enable new light to be shed on the range of contacts built up by the forerunners of the city's highly successful medieval Merchant Adventurers. For the moment, it may simply be observed that within the Anglo-Scandinavian period the economic basis of life in the city was transformed from a virtually coinless beginning to something approaching a fully-fledged money economy.

Furthermore, the production of this coinage, while not a particularly labour-intensive activity, would certainly have been of some significance. A reflection of this may be seen in the considerable status apparently enjoyed by the moneyers (Pirie 1975, lii), amongst whom a number of individuals survived the rise and fall of successive dynasties with commendable tenacity. As well as those engaged in striking coins, numbers of craftsmen were employed in cutting dies. Primary archaeological evidence for minting at York (apart from that provided by the coins themselves) is, however, limited to the single struck lead fragment referred to above (p 29) by Professor Dolley.

Conclusion

In this review an effort has been made to stress the primary evidence for commerce and for manufacturing industries respectively, but the sparse nature of the evidence often places quite severe limits on our ability to formalize to any great extent the impressions which are glimpsed in this way. But from the incontrovertible evidence which can be adduced for long-lived and long-distance trade in any one class of goods, we may deduce that similar enterprise would have been exhibited in others; not least of these would have been perishables such as butter, honey, ale, wine, and animal fodder which the city would have consumed in large quantities, and there would have been a reciprocal outflow of manufactured goods.

From contemporary documentary sources we know that the city which supported these activities was subjected periodically to siege and destruction, culminating in widespread despoliation in the course of the Norman conquest. This reconsideration of the material remains of the Anglo-Scandinavian period has revealed no trace of these dramatic events but has presented instead an abundance of material testifying to a well-ordered and industrious society. Sir Thomas Kendrick once remarked (1968, 15) that the Northman was at heart always more of a chapman than a robber, and it seems entirely appropriate that the archaeological evidence in support of this statement should be so unequivocal in the city of Jorvik, principal emporium of the Danelaw.

Acknowledgements

I am most grateful for advice given by those specialists credited in the text whose work is, as yet, unpublished. For the line drawings I am indebted to Sheena Howarth. The paper was read in draft by Mr James Graham-Campbell, many of whose observations were subsequently incorporated in the text. This contribution is largely based on the work of the York Archaeological Trust since 1972. Thanks are due for permission to make preliminary publication in advance of the definitive reports in *The Archaeology of York*.

Notes

1   For a soapstone mould from Dublin, see Ó Ríordáin 1971, 73, Fig 21d.
2   A full report by Dr Neil Berridge of the Institute of Geological Sciences, Leeds, is contained in an account of the Lloyds Bank finds in MacGregor, forthcoming.
3   The Lloyds Bank fragments were seen by several archaeologists during the excavations, but seem never to have been accessioned.
4   The petrological evidence from these finds is discussed by S E Ellis and D T Moore in MacGregor, forthcoming.
5   Mr David Brown has kindly drawn my attention to these dice. A full account of them by Mr Brown will appear in M Biddle and S Keene (editors), *Winchester Studies* 7 (forthcoming).
6   This suggestion was made to me by Mr Dick Reid. Since this paper was compiled, a twist-drill with a spiral tip has been found in a 12th-13th century context at Coppergate; this is exactly the type of implement with which a reamer *could* have been used.
7   I have discussed this hypothesis with Mr J McN Dodgson, who comments that, as far as can be discerned from the form of the name Hartergate, the allusion is to the animal or to the derived personal name rather than to the material; the discovery in the area of so much evidence for an industry based on the material remains of the animal is a remarkable coincidence, the significance of which has yet to be established.
8   Even those with unexceptional decoration have teeth cut with considerable accuracy.
9   An explanation of the working of a pole-lathe is given in Hodges 1964, 117-8. The type survived in use until the present century (Hughes 1953, 92).
10   Both scabbards from Parliament Street discussed here owe their survival to the vigilance of Mr Alan Stockdale, an amateur archaeologist from the city.
11   A scabbard from Southgate Street, Gloucester, is almost identical in design to that from Parliament Street (see *Antiq J*, 52 (1972), 61); further information from Miss Cherry Goudge.
12   Summarized from a forthcoming report by Miss Jane Holdsworth in *The Archaeology of York* **16**. I am indebted to Miss Holdsworth for allowing me access to this material in advance of her publication.

The environment of Anglo-Scandinavian York

H K Kenward, D Williams, P J Spencer, J R A Greig, D J Rackham, and D A Brinklow

Introduction

The environmental archaeologist aims to obtain information about ancient ecology, including human living conditions and behaviour, by examining biological remains and soils from archaeological sites. Environmental archaeology has only emerged as an integrated discipline during the past decade, although the remains of plants, vertebrates, and, more rarely, insects, from archaeological sites have often been catalogued in the past. Most of the early investigators simply made species lists, which appeared as appendices to excavation reports, often without reference to the main text. Modern studies have more the nature of detective work and attempt to relate closely to, and amplify, the archaeological evidence. The rather inadequate term 'environmental archaeology' embraces a number of specialist fields. Pedology, the analysis of soils (using the word to include all kinds of deposits), can give information about the nature and origin of the material forming the matrix in which the archaeological and biological evidence is preserved. It is a fundamental yet often neglected aspect of scientific archaeology. A variety of botanical remains, principally seeds, moss, timber, and pollen, commonly occur in archaeological deposits. Plant remains from urban sites mainly provide evidence of human activities, but in natural deposits or preserved soil profiles they allow reconstruction of the vegetation growing nearby. Pollen from natural deposits can be used to obtain general pictures of the vegetation of wide areas. While work on pollen from urban sites is in its infancy there is evidence that it will be valuable, for example in pinpointing the importation of certain materials. Insects, especially beetles, can provide some information about human activity but are most useful in determining past ecological conditions. This is true of urban as well as rural sites because insects exploit a wide range of habitats including those, like rotting vegetation or stored food, created by man and because, unlike plants, they were not likely to have been deliberately brought on to sites. Vertebrate remains may exceptionally give some insight into local ecology, but are most important in providing evidence of human diet and activity. Combining the results of two or more of these disciplines often greatly clarifies the information retrieved. For example, soil analysis of an occupation layer within a building may indicate the origin of the matrix, while the plants may provide evidence of the materials imported into the building, diet, and activity, and the insects may indicate the conditions within it; but when these lines of evidence are combined they will overlap and interlock so as to clarify and cross check each other.

The city of York is especially suitable for research in environmental archaeology, firstly because widespread waterlogging provides suitable conditions for the preservation of organic material, and secondly because it has been an important urban settlement, the centre of northern England, from the Roman period onward. Little work has been published concerning its past environment. Plant remains from the Hungate excavation were described by Godwin

& Bachem (1959) but the evidence recovered was of limited value. The publication of a preliminary speculative account of the plant and insect remains from the Anglo-Scandinavian site at Lloyds Bank, 6-8 Pavement, marked the first attempt at a close integration of biological evidence from an archaeological site (Buckland *et al* 1974). Buckland (1973, 1974) has briefly discussed some aspects of the past environment of York and the Vale of York, while Radley & Simms (1970) have reviewed the evidence concerning flooding and the tidal regime in the Ouse and Humber. Radley (1971) made use of some biological evidence in his paper on economic aspects of Anglo-Danish York. Unfortunately much of this early work is based on very limited evidence or is primarily speculative. In this paper we will attempt to evaluate the existing evidence concerning the ancient environment of York and its rural surroundings and to indicate what can realistically be hoped for in the future from biological studies. For this purpose the evidence will be discussed under two main headings: (i) the regional environment and (ii) conditions and activities within the town. Two other aspects of the environment of ancient York—flooding and climate—will also be briefly considered.

The regional environment

Vegetation

The settlement at York originated with the establishment *c* AD 71-4 of a Roman legionary fortress (*Eburacum*) on strategically important raised ground near the confluence of the rivers Foss and Ouse (RCHMY 1). The development of the city since that time has depended upon the character of its surroundings, for example, vegetation, soils, and topography, as well as upon the influence of successive waves of migrating peoples. Our knowledge of the regional vegetation in the early historical periods will be largely dependent on pollen analysis, which is only at a preliminary stage; in addition localized and more specific information will occasionally be obtained from the study of insects and plant macrofossils. Pollen analysis of Askham Bogs, a site two miles outside the modern city, is yielding very useful results which can be compared with other radiocarbon-dated pollen diagrams from the north-east, few though they are (Bartley 1975; Bartley *et al* 1976). There are good reasons for equating the upper part of the Askham diagram (Fig 37) with the immediately post-Roman period and onwards; in particular there is a Cannabiaceae pollen curve starting at 0.39m. The pollen record for this period has abundant signs of forest clearance and agriculture, and suggests a mosaic of arable and pasture land with areas of woodland, coppice, and heathland. There is, however, not yet any quantitative or distributional evidence for the pattern of land use.

As so little is known from biological studies it is useful to examine the documentary evidence. While there is scant contemporary documentation there is a great deal of

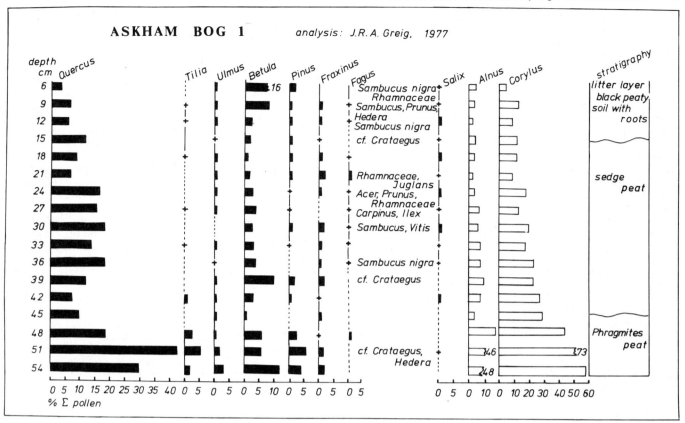

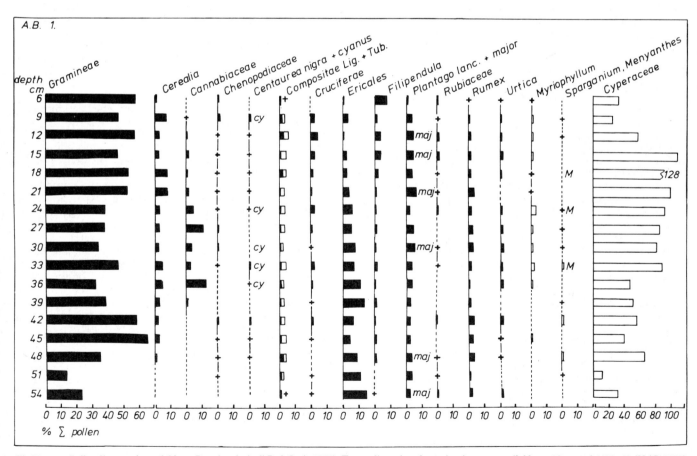

Fig 37   Pollen diagram from Askham Bogs (analysis: J R A Greig 1977). Two radio-carbon determinations are available; at 28 cms ad 1480±80 (HAR-2259) and at 50 cms bc 60±90 (HAR-2256)

medieval and later date, which for some purposes can probably be safely extrapolated back to the Anglo-Scandinavian period. The Domesday survey shows how sparsely the county was wooded (Page 1907). There are many records of the area known as the Forest of Galtres, which probably became a Royal Forest in the Norman period but is known to have been a favourite hunting ground of the Saxon kings prior to this (Cox 1905). In pre-Conquest times it was probably a belt of well-wooded country extending up the east side of the Vale of York. Its name is of Scandinavian origin, meaning 'boars' brushwood', suggesting that much of it was scrub land (Cowling 1967). It is stated that the forest started at the foot of the city walls, extended northwards for some twenty miles, and was bounded by the rivers Ouse, Kyle, and Foss (Cowling 1967, Cox 1905). However, the existence of woodland immediately adjacent to the city is unlikely, the word 'forest' referring to the area of administration of the royal hunting ground. The Forest of Galtres would probably have been an area of open woodland and parkland, broken by villages with their associated areas of tillage, grassy clearings for deer grazing, and thicker wooded areas or coverts retained strictly for game. This woodland would have been under continual pressure from grazing animals, swine pannage, assarting, and the felling of trees for building and fuel.

Plant macrofossils recovered from urban archaeological deposits are more suited to providing evidence of human activity than of the surrounding environment. Nevertheless, the regular occurrence of large amounts of certain plants in deposits in York strongly suggests that they grew close to the city. Some idea of the surrounding vegetation can thus be obtained. There is an abundance of ling (*Calluna vulgaris* (L.) Hull) in post-Roman to early medieval deposits, indicating that there was extensive heathland not too far from the town. Further evidence is provided by large quantities of typical heathland mosses, doubtless imported, found in excavations at 21-3 Aldwark (Seaward & Williams 1976) and an early medieval moss-lined pit at Skeldergate (Kenward & Williams in preparation b). *Erica* (heath) leaves, and seeds of the Scots pine (*Pinus sylvestris* L.), both typical heathland plants, were found with fragments of ling in an Anglo-Scandinavian leather-workers' tenement at 6-8 Pavement (Kenward & Williams in preparation a). In general, ling and moss would have been put to fairly unspecialized uses, such as flooring, bedding, or roofing, and it would have been uneconomical to transport them over great distances. Heathland was, therefore, probably much nearer the city in these early historical periods than are the present day vestiges such as Skipwith Common. This is supported by references to extensive heathland close to the city until comparatively late historical times (Page 1907). The heaths have now been largely obliterated by development and their reclamation for agriculture or amenity areas. Birch and pine recolonization of these heaths in the early historical periods, as today, was probably hampered by human activity.

Marshland plants are strongly represented in Anglo-Scandinavian and early medieval deposits in York. This is doubtless due to the importation of large quantities of the reed (*Phragmites communis* Trin.), tall growing sedges (*Carex* species), and to a lesser extent rushes (*Juncus* species). These materials would have been gathered mainly for thatching and flooring; the latter usage seems probable in the case of the Anglo-Scandinavian floors found under Lloyds Bank, 6-8 Pavement. Marshland would have been extensive in low lying areas of York, particularly at the confluence of the rivers. There is documentary evidence

for its presence in the Hungate area as late as the 12th century (Richardson 1959) and there is macrofossil and pollen evidence for marsh, in situ, from the excavation at 21-3 Aldwark. During the collection of reeds and sedges the accidental gathering of other marsh plants would be inevitable and the seed remains found in occupation deposits present a typical flora of the habitat. Ragged robin (*Lychnis flos-cuculi* L.), marsh marigold (*Caltha palustris* L.), yellow flag (*Iris pseudacorus* L.) and meadow sweet (*Filipendula ulmaria* (L.) Maxim.) represent water margins; these lead into the reed-swamp proper, with reed (*Phragmites communis*) and sedge (*Cladium mariscus* (L.) Pohl). There are usually very few true aquatic species; water-crowfoot (*Ranunculus*, subgenus *Batrachium*) and duckweed (*Lemna* species) have been recorded. The pressure on marsh must have been considerable near a town as large as York even if reeds and sedges were only collected for thatch, but there also would have been a need for land reclamation as the town expanded. Thus one may envisage the rapid recession of marshland from the margins of the built-up area until it was confined to the Foss Ings by the 18th century (Fife & Walls 1973); the process would have been temporarily reversed by deliberate flooding to form the castle moat in the Norman period. The cropping of reeds and sedges would have largely prevented colonization by trees and the development of alder carr. However, the predominant use of alder wood for wattle stakes and the like at 6-8 Pavement suggests a readily available source of this tree, and some alder carr probably existed on land bordering the two rivers. Wetland habitats, including the alder carr, were strongly represented on the River Ouse until quite recent times (Radley & Simms 1970).

The insects found in archaeological deposits in York can add little to the picture of the countryside already established, for most of them probably originated in the town. However, a few species are believed to have been accidentally imported, alive or dead, by human beings, some perhaps in silt and others with plants. In addition, many insects probably arrived on the wing or in the droppings of birds which had been feeding outside the town. These have been called 'background fauna' as they are irrelevant when conditions on the spot are being investigated (Kenward 1975b; 1976a), but for the present purposes they are of some value as evidence of conditions in the surroundings. Only a few insects from natural habitats occur regularly in archaeological deposits in York and with a single exception they are aquatic and waterside species. The true aquatics found in Anglo-Scandinavian and early medieval layers can be divided into two main groups; those of still or sluggish water, mostly capable of living in marshland, (Dytiscidae and Hydrophilidae) and those from running water (Elminthidae), with the former much more abundant. Insects from marshland would inevitably have been introduced with reeds and waterside mud used on the sites and may also have arrived in large numbers in the background fauna. Species which breed in mud at the edge of water are fairly common in Viking-age deposits and one, *Platystethus nitens* (Sahlb.), occurs with particular regularity. Most of the insects associated with mud and aquatic-emergent or waterside vegetation might have been living in marshy river edges, but two beetles, *Trechus secalis* (Payk.) and *Dromius longiceps* Dej. are more typical of fen and carr. *Anotylus nitidulus* (Grav.) is a small beetle often abundant in Anglo-Scandinavian and medieval deposits. It lives in various habitats but apparently reaches the greatest numbers in swamps, for example Wicken Fen, Cambs (Ormer-Cooper & Tottenham 1934), so those found in York may have been derived from large populations in the marshes nearby.

Although a number of terrestrial plant-feeding beetles have been found at 6-8 Pavement and 5 Coppergate, most could have lived on weedy wasteland in the town. However, one, *Strophosomus sus* St., recorded from several layers, is a typical heathland weevil and may well have been imported with ling.

All that it is possible to deduce from such imported species is that their habitats probably existed near to the town, and they can contribute little to our knowledge of the surrounding countryside.

In summary, it would appear that in the Anglo-Scandinavian period the countryside around York was extensively deforested and largely agricultural, a mixture of arable and pastureland, with areas of woodland, some exploited for timber or as coppice. There were probably wastelands and woodland primarily used for hunting, and extensive heaths and marshes, the latter very close to the town. A fuller picture of ecology and land use could be obtained by examining plant and insect remains from a wide range of natural and rural archaeological deposits, feasible only in the long term.

Agriculture

The extent to which new agricultural and animal husbandry practices were introduced by the Viking settlers remains uncertain. Since geography is the prime influence upon settlement and agriculture, and given the eclectic nature attributed to the Scandinavians (Wilson 1976a), the settlement might be expected to have produced only limited changes in the farming practices developed over the previous several centuries. The Scandinavians may have opened up some hitherto uncultivated tracts of land (Oldfield 1963; Pennington 1970) and increased the density of settlement in some areas (Wilson 1968b; 1976a; b); for an alternative view see Sawyer, above p 7).

The plant macrofossil evidence from York does suggest distinct differences between Anglo-Scandinavian agriculture and that of earlier periods, particularly the Roman, even allowing for the contrasting nature of the deposits. However, these differences are not necessarily related entirely to local agricultural practices, for there were great changes in the pattern and extent of trade. For example, spelt (*Triticum spelta* L.), the predominant cereal crop of the Romans, comprised 60% of the charred grain deposit at Coney Street, York (Kenward & Williams in press), while oat (*Avena sativa* L.) grain predominated in the Anglo-Scandinavian levels at 6-8 Pavement. There is, however, evidence that the Roman grain was imported from the south-east of Britain or even the continent, while Anglo-Scandinavian cereals were probably locally grown. It has been suggested by Godwin (1975) that the records of oats in East Anglia may reflect the introduction of the crop by migrating Saxon peoples, so this change at least was perhaps unrelated to the Vikings. The cereal weed stinking mayweed (*Anthemis cotula* L.) is very characteristic of Anglo-Scandinavian and early medieval deposits in York. Its achenes were found in large numbers dispersed with charred grain in the 6-8 Pavement occupation layers, for example. This plant grows predominantly on clay or clay-loam soils, particularly if they are base-rich (Kay 1971). The present-day abundance of stinking mayweed on the heavier soils of the Weald of Kent, areas first cultivated by the Anglo-Saxons, suggested to Kay that it would have been a troublesome cereal weed in the past—this was certainly the case around York.

The pollen evidence from Askham Bogs suggests that cereals were grown close to York throughout post-Roman times. The very high values of cereal pollen together with unspecific types such as the Compositae at the 6-8 Pavement site may reflect the importation of straw or grain with adhering pollen, rather than local large scale cultivation of grain crops (Robinson & Hubbard 1977). Stinking mayweed achenes may have been introduced in the same way.

Two other crops strongly represented in post-Roman York and doubtless grown locally are hemp (*Cannabis sativa* L.) and flax (*Linum usitatissimum* L.). Hemp seeds were very common throughout the deposits below 6-8 Pavement and have also been recovered in appreciable numbers from other Anglo-Scandinavian and early medieval deposits, for example at 5 Coppergate. The palynological evidence from Askham Bogs shows a strong hemp curve, indicative of local cultivation. Since the plant was apparently present in the north-east in the Iron Age (Bartley *et al* 1976) the increased abundance of hemp seeds in post-Roman deposits at York could be due to differences in the pattern of preservation in the two periods rather than an increase in the use of the plant. There is pollen evidence for Romano-British hemp cultivation in other areas, for example Skelsmergh Tarn, Westmorland and Lindow Moss, Cheshire (Godwin 1967a; 1967b). However, at other sites such as Old Buckenham Mere, East Anglia it was not established until the Anglo-Saxon period, becoming very important in Viking and Norman times (Godwin 1967b). Hemp cultivation was also common in the Tudor period, when it was enforced by law to ensure adequate provision of cordage for the navy (Godwin 1975).

Pollen of the family Cruciferae is abundant in the Askham Bogs diagram, but unfortunately it cannot be identified to species; the group includes many weeds, for example white charlock (*Raphanus raphanistrum* L.), as well as crops. Abundant finds of the distinctively ribbed fruit of white charlock in all periods suggests that this cereal weed was as common in the past as it is today. On the other hand a variety of crucifer crops might have been grown, such as mustard (*Sinapsis alba* L.), gold of pleasure (*Camelina sativa* (L.) Crantz) grown for oil seed, or woad (*Isatis tinctoria* L.) grown for dye, which would all have been allowed to flower and liberate pollen before harvest. Flowering, and thus pollen production, is most undesirable before harvesting crops such as cabbage (*Brassica oleracea* L.) and turnips (*Brassica rapa* L.) and there is a dearth of evidence for these plants as a result. However, seeds tentatively identified as turnip or swede have frequently been recovered and are probably the product of small-scale horticultural activities. There are somewhat scattered records of pollen attributable to *Vicia* or its close relatives. This could represent either the field bean (*Vicia faba* L.), the pea (*Pisum sativum* L.), or wild vetch species. The seeds of leguminous crops decay rapidly, and this may be why finds of peas and beans are rare. They may be preserved by charring, however, as were a number of seeds of *Vicia faba* from 6-8 Pavement; the size of these suggests that they were the product of deliberate cultivation. Pulses may have been imported for their value as easily stored protein-rich food, so these records are not conclusive evidence of local cultivation. An early medieval moss-lined pit at Skeldergate seems, from initial examination, to have been used for pulse storage, or perhaps the disposal of spoiled seed (Kenward & Williams in preparation b).

Detailed reconstruction of the pattern of past agriculture, as of natural vegetation, demands biological studies of rural deposits. However, there is evidence from work on urban York of the cultivation of a range of crops, particularly

cereals and hemp. Many other plants were apparently
exploited, although there is no evidence for their
deliberate cultivation (see above). The degree to which
the Scandinavians altered agricultural practices is uncertain.
We are almost wholly ignorant of the conditions in Anglian
Yorkshire, and have a limited knowledge of the Viking
period, but there is evidence for some changes in farming at
about the time of the Scandinavian settlement. Further
aspects of agriculture and the utilization of plant and
animal resources are discussed below.

Environment and human activity in the town

The archaeological evidence, in the strict sense, can only
give limited information about the appearance of the
town and living conditions in it. The archaeologists'
unconfirmed identification of, for example, a 'clay' floor or
a 'layer of reeds' may form the basis of various assumptions,
sometimes poorly reasoned, as to what sites were really like
in the past. Many of the accepted ideas of archaeology are
based on such assumptions and its increasingly scientific
outlook will probably lead to some of these ideas being
greatly revised. The environmental archaeologist can test
and amplify the conclusions drawn by the archaeologist
from observations during excavation and produce a wide
range of information unobtainable except by laboratory
analysis. If the conventional excavation evidence is examined
with a sceptical eye, surprisingly few definite conclusions
about life and conditions in Viking-age York can be drawn.
For example, deliberately-laid floors are often covered by
thick accumulations of organic debris, but the archaeological
evidence does not tell us whether this was laid down
during occupation or after abandonment; holes were dug
and organic refuse put into them, but it is not possible to
say whether this was the primary function of a pit or
merely a way of filling it in after use for industrial or
storage purposes. Little more can be said with certainty
on the evidence from other towns, even Novgorod or
Hedeby where streets and whole ground plans have been
found in excavations covering very large areas. While
it is probably unfair to examine the archaeological evidence
quite so sceptically, it must be remembered that it is,
together with documentary fragments and tenuous folk
parallels, the basis of our view of the period. It is most
important that biological data should not be simply hung
on to these preconceived ideas, often leading to circular
arguments; rather, all the evidence must be examined
with an open mind, so as to arrive at logical conclusions.
This point may be illustrated by two examples. Dyer's
rocket (*Reseda luteola* L.) has been found on a number of
occasions in Anglo-Scandinavian York and medieval Hull
(Miller *et al* in press). This is not, however, proof that
dyeing was carried out on the sites, because the plant is
an arable weed of calcareous soils and there is good evidence
from these sites of the importation of cereals from areas
with such soils. The eyeless beetle *Aglenus brunneus* (Gyll.)
was often found in tanneries in the 19th century, and is very
common in archaeological sites where there are remains of
leather. It has many other habitats, however, and cannot be
used as evidence of tanning, being merely compatible
with it (Kenward 1975a; 1976b). Nevertheless, by cautious
examination of the evidence it is possible to obtain a great
deal of information.

In this discussion the biological evidence concerning life
in urban York will be examined from two viewpoints.
Firstly, what activities were carried out by the townspeople?
Secondly, what was the state of the town as a result of
these activities?

Human activity
Importation of materials

The importation of materials was one of the most important
factors determining conditions within the town. Materials
are brought on to occupation sites for various reasons,
some, like soils, simply to be used in their initial state and
others, for example dye-plants, skins, or antler, to be used
in complex craft and industrial activities. Sometimes the
imported material itself is preserved, for example silt,
timber, and layers of ling or reeds. More often there is no
direct evidence and some laboratory detective work is
required before it is shown that a particular material
was used.

Soils were very obviously transported on a large scale,
both in the disposal of spoil and for embanking or making
packed floors. While clean clays and silts may occasionally
have been brought from outside the town, for daub or
lining pits for example, it is quite likely that material for
unspecialized uses would be obtained simply by digging
within it or as a by-product of excavating trenches and pits.
Evidence from 6-8 Pavement suggests that most of the
soil for floors was obtained from local build-up (Hood, pers
comm), although a few layers seem to have
incorporated mud from marshland (Kenward & Williams
in preparation a). There is little reason to suppose that
the rapid rate of build-up was a deliberate response to
flooding or a high water table. A large part of the 5m of
accumulation at 6-8 Pavement was probably due to organic
material thrown on to the floors during occupation.

Timber was a major import, used for many purposes,
and is often well preserved. There was rigid selection of
trees according to the intended use. For example, larger
timbers used in building construction were oak, chosen
for strength and durability. Young, flexible twigs of birch
and alder were used for wattle and pegs. Bowls were
generally turned from ash and occasionally from other
fine-grained woods; alder turning bases found in York
provide evidence that bowls were made within the town.
Some trees were used on a small scale for very specialized
purposes. Skewers, pins, and combs for example, are often
of yew, selected for its hardness.

Vast amounts of plant material were brought into
Anglo-Scandinavian York and a large proportion of the
build-up is derived from rotting plant matter, as attested by
its highly organic, even peaty, nature and by the insect
remains it contains (p 65).

Ling and tall waterside vegetation appear to have been
introduced in the greatest bulk. This was probably used
for such unspecialized purposes as bedding, flooring,
and thatching. There is also a hint from pollen evidence,
supported by certain seeds, that straw or hay was imported.
What these materials were used for has not yet been
certainly determined; it is hoped that excavation at 16-22
Coppergate will provide an opportunity to solve many
such problems.

Industry

The Coppergate and Pavement area of York has been
referred to as the industrial centre of the Anglo-Scandinavian
town (Radley 1971), and there is an increasing amount of
biological evidence to support this. The large number of
records of hemp and flax from this area has already been
mentioned. These plants were almost certainly grown for

their fibres and probably formed the basis of a flourishing textile industry in York, producing coarse fabrics and rope from the hemp, and linen from the flax, although as yet no clear evidence of textile manufacture has been found on any site. There is some evidence fom 6-8 Pavement compatible with dyeing, presumably of textiles. Several dye plants are recorded, for example Dyer's rocket (*Reseda luteola* L.). *Apion difficile* Hbst., a weevil found on dyer's greenweed, *Genista tinctoria* L., has been recorded from several layers. The young tips of shoots and florets of ling have also been found. The absence of larger stems and shoots of this extremely robust plant suggests deliberate selection of its upper parts, which have been used to produce a yellow dye. Extremely large numbers of elder seeds were also found with these dye plants, particularly with *Reseda*, but while elder could have been used for tanning as suggested by Buckland *et al* (1974) or even as a dye or mordant, it is just as likely to have had a culinary use. Teasel (*Dipsacus fullonum* L.), a plant cultivated in gardens in the medieval period to meet the needs of fullers and cloth-workers (Gerarde 1636), was also recovered from these deposits.

Domestic animals had great importance in the Viking-age economy, both as a food resource and as the basis of several major industries. Apart from work on material from Hedeby and Lund (Ekman 1973; Reichstein 1969; Reichstein & Tiessen 1974), no intensive analysis of the animal bones from Scandinavian Viking-age urban sites has yet been published. In the British Isles the only major Viking towns being excavated on any scale are Dublin, York, and Lincoln. A characteristic of these towns, and Viking settlements in Continental Europe, is the abundant evidence of commercial and industrial activity making use of animal materials such as bone, antler, leather, fur, and wool. Such activities were, however, by no means the sole preserve of the urban centres in which they were concentrated, evidence for them occurring commonly on all types of settlement (eg Hamilton 1956).

Excavations in York have given various indications of the craft industries of the Anglo-Scandinavian town. Bone was used in the manufacture of a number of items (pp 46-8) and there is evidence of a considerable industry using antler. At 5 Coppergate, for example, large numbers of fragments were found and antler working was probably carried out commercially on the site. Almost all the combs found in York have been of red deer antler. Radley (1971, 48) suggested that whole carcasses were brought into York, but at present the evidence suggests that shed antlers were normally used. The use of horn is strikingly illustrated by the medieval waste pit at Hornpot Lane (Ryder 1970), but the only find of the Anglo-Scandinavian period is a quantity of horn cores, mainly of ox, but with some goat and sheep, from 5 Coppergate. These cores had been sawn or chopped from the skulls and so had obviously been deliberately retained. Bone, horn, and antler industries and their products are of course well known throughout the Viking world, but work at York has not progressed to the point where worthwhile comparisons with other centres can be made.

There is much evidence of a thriving leatherworking industry at York, recently reviewed by Radley (1971); further data have come from the excavation at 6-8 Pavement, (Addyman 1975a, 221) and for the early medieval period from 16-22 Coppergate. While these finds of vast quantities of leather off-cuts clearly indicate that leatherworking was important at least in the Coppergate-Pavement area, there is little evidence that hides were actually prepared in the town and indeed it could be argued that such a foul-smelling activity may not have been tolerated within the main part of the settlement. The leather which has been identified to date has been of ox and calf, and possibly deer skin from Hungate (Richardson 1959, 90). Botanical evidence for a textile industry has been considered above. A few pieces of woollen cloth and yarn have been discovered; analysis of wool from 6-8 Pavement (Ryder in press) shows it to be of the 'medium' and 'hairy' types typical of the Viking periods of north-east England and Scotland.

Food

There is growing evidence of the food plants consumed by the Anglo-Scandinavians. These range from those collected in the wild, such as blackberry and hazelnuts (shell fragments of the latter were very common at 6-8 Pavement), through such common, possibly cultivated plants as carrot, celery, apple, brassicas, and stone fruits (*Prunus* species) to more specialized crops such as the field bean (*Vicia faba* L.). These, together with cereal cultivation, have been discussed on p 61.

Certain species could have had medicinal use, for example henbane (*Hyoscyamus niger* L.), white bryony (*Bryonia dioica* Jacq.) and agrimony (*Agrimonia eupatoria* L.). These occur frequently in small numbers but it is not certain that they were deliberately collected because many, such as henbane, occurred commonly as weeds near human habitation until recent times. However, reference to early herbals shows just how widespread was the use of such plants, many of which, for example mugwort (*Artemesia vulgaris* L.), had more mystical than medical value (Grigson 1958).

Most bones found on archaeological sites are leftovers from food and this is as true of Viking-age York as of elsewhere. The relative numbers of different food animals and the kind of bones present on a site can give some indication of the quality of diet and thus perhaps the degree of affluence of the occupants. The proportion of the various domestic animals from some sites in York is shown in Fig 38. During the Anglo-Scandinavian period the domestic remains, representative of diet, are predominantly of cattle, which generally seem to have been killed when they had reached three or more years of age. The relatively low numbers of distal ends of the lower limb bones from the excavation at 5 Coppergate (Hall 1976b) may mean that the meat was bought ready butchered. Studies of bones may give an underestimation of the importance of pig in the diet, for apart from jaws their bones are generally poorly preserved. Pig remains were abundant in Dublin, where it has been suggested that the animals may have helped clear up the domestic refuse (Anon 1973). Sheep appear to have been less important in the diet than pig on the basis of evidence from 6-8 Pavement, and the majority were mature or over two years of age when killed. Goat bones have been found on several sites in York, but in small numbers. There are, however, problems in distinguishing their skeletons from those of sheep so their numbers may be underestimated. Goat horn cores of a large sabre-like type found at York (Radley 1971, 48) could represent a Scandinavian introduction. Goats may have been imported for their meat or skins, or perhaps were kept by the inhabitants of the town for their milk.

Fowl and domestic goose bones are common on some sites (Dyer & Wenham 1958; Rackham, D J, in preparation). The discovery of almost complete chicken skeletons in pits at 6-8 Pavement, together with the occurrence of eggshell, down, and feathers (Buckland *et al* 1974) suggests

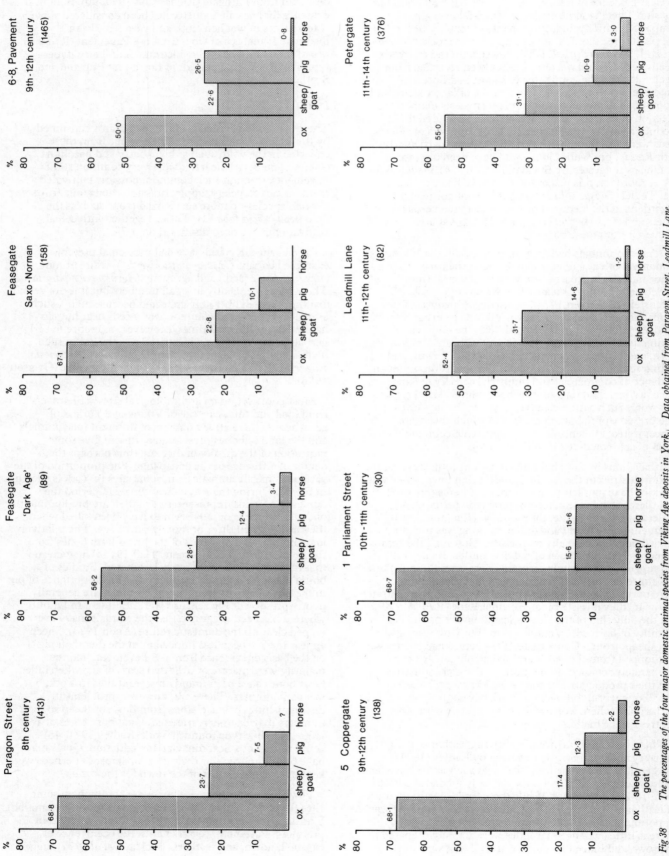

Fig 38   *The percentages of the four major domestic animal species from Viking Age deposits in York.. Data obtained from Paragon Street, Leadmill Lane, 6-8 Pavement, and 5 Coppergate (Rackham, unpublished); Feasegate (Dyer and Wenham 1958); 1 Parliament Street (Bramwell, pers comm); 65 Low Petergate (Ryder 1970). *Part of three horse skeletons found. Numbers in parentheses are totals of bones per site.*

that chickens may have been kept in the town; they and their eggs would have formed a convenient source of cheap protein.

Wild animals are poorly known in York. Hare, white-fronted goose, wild duck, cormorant, and plover bones were found at 6-8 Pavement, perhaps offering a little evidence of a supplement to the main diet. Fish, both freshwater and marine, may have been more important in the diet than the records of bones and scales indicate because of difficulties in recovering them. Cod has been identified from 6-8 Pavement (Wheeler, pers comm) and also from the 16-22 Coppergate excavation. A remarkable layer of remains of small herrings was found on the site of St Mary Bishophill Junior (Cramp 1967); it is estimated that between one and two thousand fish were represented. This and other evidence has been used to suggest that the site had been used for fish processing, presumably commercially. The failure to recover other species of fish is surprising, especially in view of the location of the city on two rivers and close to the Humber. It seems that large-scale sieving of soil during excavation, now in progress, will produce much more evidence of fish in the diet. Shellfish are abundant in the Anglo-Scandinavian layers at York. Oysters are most common, but cockles, whelks, and mussels are also found.

Overall, a picture emerges of a busy industrious people with a varied diet who obtained materials from a wide area. For example, sainfoin, *Onobrychis viciifolia* Scop., and other species requiring a base-rich soil probably came from the Wolds, many miles away, while marine fish and shellfish were brought from the coast. However, there are some hints that trade in food plants occurred over even greater distances. Walnut, for example, has been recovered from the excavations at 16-22 Coppergate. Further work should give much more information about the transport and trade of foodstuffs and industrial raw materials.

Conditions within the town

It seems that organic material, both plant and animal, formed the basis of almost every aspect of Anglo-Scandinavian daily life and that this material sooner or later became incorporated into the rapidly accumulating layers of debris on which the town was built. Ecological conditions were almost entirely determined by human activity, probably incidentally rather than deliberately. By establishing which plants and animals could find suitable habitats it should be possible to find out a great deal about the appearance of Viking-age York and the conditions endured by its occupants.

The remains of insects, especially beetles, will provide the best evidence of ecological conditions, and thus the human environment, within the town. In contrast to the plants they had no obvious economic value and so were not deliberately imported. Insects exploit a very wide range of habitats, including those created by man, and so can be used to determine conditions even in buildings and yards where plants could not live. Beetles were clearly abundant throughout the known part of the Anglo-Scandinavian and medieval town, having been found wherever preservational conditions were suitable; several hundred species have been identified from deposits in York. The most abundant or regularly occurring species are listed with their habitat preferences in Fig 39. Remains of many of the species are present in most samples large enough to give an adequate representation of the nearby fauna and their absence from the smaller ones is probably only a matter of chance. Many more are fairly often recorded and were

without a doubt established in the town. The overall impression is of extremely uniform groups of insect remains ('death assemblages') and this is also true of other urban settlements, including Durham, Hull, and Dublin. Most of the beetle assemblages from these towns are indistinguishable from those at York, although not enough work has been done to be sure there are no subtle constant differences.

In addition to beetles, houseflies and their relatives were very common. Their puparia are almost always present and often extremely abundant; some thin layers on the site at 16-22 Coppergate are entirely composed of them. Other insects, like plant bugs (Hemiptera), earwigs (*Forficula auricularia* L.), bees (probably including *Apis*, the honeybee), ants, and various parasitic wasps are often found, and a human flea (*Pulex irritans* L.) has been recovered from 6-8 Pavement.

Deciding what precise ecological conditions are indicated by these insect death assemblages is a difficult problem because of the diverse origin of the fauna recovered from most samples (Kenward 1975b; 1976a), and it is not feasible to describe the methods here. Using some specialized techniques it is often possible to obtain quite detailed information (Kenward in press a), but for the present purposes a very general outline of the overall implications of the several hundred Anglo-Scandinavian and medieval assemblages so far examined will be attempted. The more abundant and regularly occurring beetles fall into five groups:
a) some water beetles and waterside species (see p 60)
b) the vast majority, associated with decaying organic matter or at least most abundant in such habitats
c) a number of species associated with decaying wood
d) a few species now regarded as domestic or storage pests
e) a few species associated with outdoor urban habitats

Most of the species falling in the last three groups are not quite common enough to appear in Fig 39.

The majority of the beetles listed are most abundant in rotting organic matter or are even confined to it. There is evidence that such species were breeding in, or close to, many of the layers which have been examined for insect remains, and rotting organic matter appears to have been the predominant insect habitat in the known part of the town. Many species occur in very large numbers, for example 160 *Aglenus brunneus* (Gyll.) in a sample of 5 kg from 6-8 Pavement; these are undoubtedly the corpses of populations breeding in the material which rotted away to form the sampled layer. Species which regularly occur in smaller numbers may have been breeding without becoming abundant, or be stray individuals which originated some distance from the deposits in which they were found. Some *Anotylus*, *Oxytelus*, and *Platystethus* species are probably often strays, while some large predators like *Philonthus* species and ground beetles were probably breeding but relatively rare.

Many of the compost insects were doubtless exploiting pits and middens, where their corpses are regularly present, but they are also abundant in layers regarded as internal floors, for example at 6-8 Pavement. It appears that they were able to breed in large numbers within buildings, suggesting that the plants found preserved in many layers were strewn on floors and left to rot there. This has not yet, however, been proved conclusively; indeed, 'occupation build-up' might be material dumped during the periods between structural phases. Compost beetles can, very crudely, be divided into two groups: those which tolerate foul moist conditions, for example slimy rotting

	6-8 Pavement		5 Coppergate	Saddler St, Durham	Main habitats
	Trench II	Trench IV			
Total number of samples	27	13	18	6	
Carabidae					
Pterostichus melanarius (Ill.) * + ?	8	4	3	2	Ground beetle of catholic tastes; often associated with man
Hydrophilidae					
Helophorus spp. (small, including *brevipalpis* Bed.)	11	6	11	6	Still or sluggish water
Cercyon analis (Payk.)	20	7	18	6	Compost, haystack refuse etc
C. pygmaeus (Ill.)*	5	1	14	5	Dung, moist rotting matter
C. unipunctatus (L.)	4	3	14	2	Dung, moist rotting matter
Histeridae					
Acritus nigricornis (Hoffm.)	11	6	11	2	Rotting vegetation, stack refuse etc
Gnathoncus spp. (including *schmidti* Reit.) A	11	3	1	1	Rotting organic matter, nests
Hydraenidae					
Ochthebius spp. including *O. minimus* (F.)	11	4	1	-	Still or sluggish water
Ptiliidae					
Ptenidium spp. A	17	8	4	5	Common in compost, under seaweed etc
Staphylinidae					
Xylodromus concinnus (Msh.)	26	11	14	6	Mouldy vegetable refuse
Carpelimus bilineatus (St.) + ?	23	9	13	2	Marshy places, at grass roots etc
Platystethus arenarius (Fourcr.)	13	9	16	6	Dung, foul rotting matter
P. cornutus group, including *degener* Muls. & Rey	16	10	13	2	Waterside mud; *degener* possibly can breed in organic rich damp soil
P. nitens (Sahlb.)	14	4	7	3	Moist ground and mud
Anotylus complanatus (Er.)	18	7	17	5	Foul decaying matter, dung
A. nitidulus (Grav.)	18	10	16	5	Decaying matter; waterside mud; swamps
A. rugosus (F.)	24	12	14	5	Rotting matter, dung, mud by water
Oxytelus sculptus Grav.	13	9	15	4	Dung, moist rotting matter
Stenus spp., including *crassus* St. A	18	8	11	5	*Stenus* spp.—very wide range of habitats; *crassus* in mouldering plant matter
Leptacinus pusillus (St.) + ?	10	9	16	5	Decaying plant matter
Gyrohypnus fracticornis (Müll.)	18	8	12	4	Decaying plant matter
Neobisnius sp. (? *cerrutii* Grid.)	13	10	11	3	*N.* spp; marshy places, by water; in compost
Philonthus spp. A	20	10	16	6	Wide range of habitats; many in rotting matter
Aleocharinae indet spp. A	26	12	17	6	Very wide range of habitats, many in rotting matter
Trogidae					
Trox scaber (L.)	12	7	8	-	Dry carcasses; nests; wood mould; probably some kinds of compost
Scarabaeidae					
Aphodius prodromus (Brahm) * + ?	11	4	10	4	Dung, but often in rotting vegetation
Anobiidae					
Anobium punctatum (Deg.)	18	8	10	2	Dead wood, often in buildings
Ptinidae					
Ptinus fur (L.) *	15	5	12	1	Birds' nests; common in houses and stores
Rhizophagidae					
Monotoma spp., including *spinicollis* Aubé, *picipes* Hb. *bicolor* Villa and *longicollis* (Gyll.)	19	8	12	3	Named species all primarily found in mouldy compost
Cryptophagidae					
Cryptophagus spp. A	25	10	18	6	Wide range of habitats; many in buildings; mouldy plant matter
Atomaria spp. A	24	10	17	6	Wide range of habitats; very abundant in mouldy plant matter
Lathridiidae					
Lathridius minutus (L.) group	24	9	17	5	In mouldy compost, old straw, moss etc
Enicmus transversus (Ol.) group	19	7	2	1	In mouldy compost, old straw, moss etc
Corticaria or *Corticarina* spp. A	20	7	13		Most abundant in fairly dry decaying plant matter
Colydiidae					
Aglenus brunneus (Gyll.)	23	10	12	5	Mouldering organic matter
Anthicidae					
Anthicus formicarius (Gz.) and *floralis* (L.)	12	5	7	5	Mouldering plant matter, especially old straw
Chrysomelidae					
Phyllotreta nemorum (L.) or *undulata* Kuts.	5	4	12	2	On cruciferous plants; a pest of some crops

*Fig 39   The most abundant and regularly occurring beetles in Anglo-Scandinavian and early medieval York and Durham. * number of records from some sites probably underestimated due to problems of identification; A—compound taxa dominated by one or two species; +?—includes probables. Nomenclature follows Kloet & Hincks 1977*

grass cuttings, and are often also found in dung; and those which live in dryer plant matter, which is usually mouldy and more open-textured, for example straw or dry grass cuttings. Whether the organic matter on the floors of Viking-age buildings was wet or dry during decay would obviously be important to the occupants. The habitat preferences of compost beetles are hard to determine from the published literature but the commonest species in the floors at 6-8 Pavement seem to be those preferring dryish mouldering plant matter, 'sweet compost'; many might even have been living in thatch or mouldering wattle and daub as well as floors. This fauna is compatible with the development of the layers during occupation rather than desertion. Such species are also common in the samples from 5 Coppergate where, however, the beetles associated with foul decaying matter are present in larger numbers. This accords with the possibility that at least some of the samples from the 5 Coppergate site were from external layers, where filthier conditions were tolerable. One of a small group of samples from Saddler Street, Durham had foul compost species in great abundance, giving some guide to the fauna to be expected from damp middens, and similar assemblages have been found in a few of the medieval samples from 16-22 Coppergate. Systematic working of the insect remains from the latter site promises a much fuller picture of living conditions in the town and a clearer understanding of the communities of insects involved.

A number of wood-destroying beetles, of which *Anobium punctatum* (Deg.), the 'woodworm', is by far the most abundant, have been found in Anglo-Scandinavian and early medieval deposits. The 'powder post beetle' *Lyctus linearis* (Gz.) is also regularly found. These species could have caused a considerable amount of damage, but wet rot of the timbers where they entered the ground, surrounded by compost, would have probably been the limiting factor in the life of the buildings. The length of time that buildings could stand is obviously of considerable interest. The multiplicity of floor layers at 6-8 Pavement may be related to successive rebuildings, perhaps, to judge from analysis of the insect remains, with an alternation of packed floors and occupation build-up. A rough estimate suggests that each cycle may have taken a few decades at most.

Two longhorn beetles from 6-8 Pavement, *Gracilia minuta* (F.) and *Phymatodes alni* (L.), bore in twigs; they probably lived in wattling, although the first also damages basketwork. Several species of beetles and bugs which live under bark have been found in small numbers. It remains to be established whether this implies the regular use of timber bearing bark, or whether these insects were imported with dead wood used for burning.

A few species which damage stored food products have been found, the grain weevil *Sitophilus granarius* (L.) and two other typical grain pests, *Oryzaephilus surinamensis* (L.) and *Cryptolestes* species being the most notable. All three occur in very small numbers, however, and give no reason to suspect that grain was stored in large quantities; nothing comparable to the massive Roman infestation at Coney Street (Hall & Kenward 1976; Kenward & Williams in press) has been found. Several less specialized beetles of stores and houses occur more often, for example *Ptinus fur* (L.) (a spider beetle), *Tenebrio obscurus* F. (one of the 'mealworms') and *Blaps lethifera* Msh., (a 'churchyard beetle'). However, many such species, now usually found in stored products, may in the past have exploited the masses of organic matter in buildings, either floors or thatching. For example, *Aglenus brunneus* (Gyll.), now mostly found in grain residues, was extremely abundant in Anglo-

Scandinavian and medieval York where it doubtless exploited mouldering organic matter in general (Kenward 1975a; 1976b).

This picture of a town composed of rotting wooden buildings with earth floors covered by decaying vegetation, surrounded by streets and yards filled by pits and middens of even fouler organic waste, is probably not too far from the truth, at least for the Coppergate/Pavement area of York. More detailed analyses of individual samples indicate that where breeding communities of insects were present they largely comprised species associated with rotting organic matter. Exploration of the higher parts of York may show differentiation into an industrial area near to the Foss and better kept areas elsewhere, but preservation is likely to be rare on dry ground or in stone buildings. The insect faunas from 16-22 Coppergate fit well into the existing picture and have fascinating variety; they promise an immense amount of new information.

Conditions within the Anglo-Scandinavian buildings at 6-8 Pavement were clearly unsavoury by modern standards but may have been tolerable, even cosy, by the standards of the time. There is in any case no evidence that people lived, rather than worked, on these ground floors. The structures may have just been workshops or, less probably, there may have been a residential upper floor.

Although many species of open-air insect have been found in York they are usually rare and as likely to be imported or 'background' fauna as to have been breeding. Species which may have been living in the town are a few ground beetles, for example *Pterostichus melanarius* (Ill.) and *Trechus quadristriatus* (Schrank), both common in suburban areas at the present day, and a few plant-feeders. Of the latter, *Phyllotreta nemorum* (L.) or *undulata* Kuts., which feed on cruciferous plants, have been found regularly and may have been living on weeds in the town. Several insects which feed on nettles (*Urtica* species) have been found fairly often but no samples have been seen which offer any clear evidence that their host was growing nearby. Nettles and other weeds may, however, have been established on thatch or turf roofs rather than at ground level; detecting plants growing in such a habitat poses novel problems.

The proportion of 'outdoor' insects, that is open air species which are not associated with wooden buildings and rotting organic matter, varies from layer to layer, and in York seems often to depend upon the amount of human importation of materials. Some samples from Durham and Hull, on the other hand, have larger percentages of outdoor insects and certainly came from deposits formed outdoors. At Saddler Street, Durham, for example, semi-natural vegetation seems to have existed close by, and most of the insects probably arrived on the wing or were even washed in with surface water. At Hull a small brackish water element, for example *Berosus spinosus* (Schoen.) and *Ochthebius marinus* (Payk.), appears in the fauna, reflecting the proximity of estuarine marshes, and there is usually a rather larger proportion of outdoor insects than at York (Kenward in press b; Miller *et al* in press). Similar layers of Anglo-Scandinavian and early medieval date are rare at York, although a few of later medieval date have been found on the 16-22 Coppergate site, where some deposits seem to have formed in yards and ditches.

The abundance of seeds of weeds and ruderals in Anglo-Scandinavian deposits might be assumed to be proof that the plants grew in the town, but this evidence needs careful scrutiny in view of the rarity of associated insects. The ground was probably greatly disturbed by trampling, the digging of pits, by chickens, and perhaps even pigs, and the result may have been a severe restriction of plant life. Some typical weeds whose seeds are regularly found in large numbers are nettles (*Urtica dioica* L. and *Urtica urens* L.), fat hen (*Chenopodium album* L.), elder (*Sambucus nigra* L.), and *Polygonum* species, particularly knotgrass (*P. aviculare* agg.). All these are plants of disturbed nitrogenous conditions so that the urban soil would have been ideal for them, and their fossil records strongly associate them with human habitation (Godwin 1975). There are some plants which are notable for their absence although this might be due to differential preservation; plantains, for example, could be expected to have grown on heavily compacted areas such as pathways.

There are problems in differentiating between ruderals and those weeds of cultivation brought into the town with grain or straw. Other plants had economic use and may have been imported. Nettle, for example, has been used for its fibre and for food. A large number of wild plants now thought of as weeds were eaten, for example fat hen (*Chenopodium album* L.), and Good King Henry (*Chenopodium bonus-henricus* L.). A species whose seeds were abundant in occupation floors at 6-8 Pavement and whose presence cannot be easily accounted for is flixweed (*Descurainia sophia* (L.) Webb ex Prantl). It may have grown close by during a period of abandonment of the building, so that the seeds, which are light and easily dispersed by wind, were blown into it.

Two pollen diagrams from within York, one from a deep trench at 21-3 Aldwark and the other from 6-8 Pavement, can be examined for evidence concerning conditions in the town. The Aldwark diagram comes from organic deposits apparently laid down in a ditch from the Roman period until the 12th century. They included occasional layers of wood or ling between layers of clayey material that could have been deposited naturally or artificially. The pollen found in this material may have been transported over a long distance by wind, or have come from plants growing in the town, or from plant material imported to York. The presence or absence of weed seeds which correspond with pollen often provides valuable information about the likely origin of the pollen itself. The pollen diagram from 6-8 Pavement comes from a series of samples from the floors of the leather workers' tenement and probably contains mainly derived pollen.

Although work is in its early stages, these diagrams can tell us something about the urban environment, especially when compared with the diagram from Askham Bogs (Fig 37). First it is necessary to estimate the importance of the aerial and imported pollen components of the two diagrams. The Aldwark diagram has much less tree pollen than that from Askham Bogs, hardly surprising as one site is urban and the other rural. Oak, together with traces of elm, lime, ash, and hornbeam, probably came from the nearest woods to the city. The relative proportions of these trees are similar to those in the Askham diagram. Birch, alder, and hazel are rather more frequent than oak in the Aldwark diagram, probably reflecting the presence of scrubby woodland very close to the city. Elder is quite frequent in the Aldwark diagram, although there are only traces from Askham. It readily colonizes abandoned land, so the pollen probably represents elder growing in or very near York; the plant is common in the modern town. This accords with the finds of seeds, elder being one of the commonest of the ruderal species.

The herbaceous pollen counts in the Aldwark diagram are much higher than in the Askham samples, especially for weeds like Cruciferae, nettles (*Urtica*), and Compositae. This could represent importation of the plants, aerial pollen,

or the urban flora. The very large amounts of Ericales pollen in the upper part of the Aldwark diagram correspond with finds of the remains of *Calluna* and this pollen is certainly imported, as probably was the cereal-type pollen. There are, however, many records of pollen from weeds and ruderals which are hard to explain fully by wind transport or importation. These include Chenopodiaceae, *Artemisia*, *Centaurea nigra*-type, Caryophyllaceae, *Polygonum*, *Rumex*, and Umbelliferae, in addition to the three mentioned above. It seems on balance that weeds existed in the town, perhaps on waste ground, in alley-ways and back yards, along property boundaries, and at the bases of wooden fences and walls.

Much that has emerged from this investigation points to a town which, by modern standards, would be regarded as intolerably squalid. The existence of such conditions is perhaps not very surprising since the economy of the town was so firmly organic-based. Whether from a human point of view conditions were really so bad, or whether there is a bias in preservation towards the less pleasant side of life, must be determined by further research. It has already been suggested that there may have been tidier quarters of the town than the Coppergate/Pavement area, perhaps with stone buildings, or at least kept a good deal drier and cleaner. Unfortunately, if such areas existed, or even if phases of cleanliness occurred in the sites already investigated, they would from their very nature be unconducive to the preservation of organic remains.

The plant and animal remains found in Anglo-Scandinavian and early medieval York, and the conditions that they indicate, contrast strongly with what is known of other periods of the town. The insect fauna of the Roman settlement is dominated by a range of domestic and pest insects which might have been found in any English town at the beginning of the present century. This relative cleanliness accords well with what we know of the way of life of the Romano-British population, but may be even more a product of the inorganic nature of the town, with its stone buildings and cobbled streets. Unfortunately we know nothing of the flora and fauna of the extra-mural settlement (*canabae*) apart from the specialized structures at 39-41 Coney Street, so it is not known whether this area of more humble buildings differed markedly from the fortress and *colonia*. The transition from the Viking-age insect fauna to that recorded by the 19th century insect collectors appears to have occurred somewhere in the 12th to 15th centuries. The installation of stone floors, tiled roofs, and improved refuse disposal were probably the most important factors influencing the insect commensals of man. There is not yet enough evidence to follow the course of this change, but there are some hints that it occurred gradually and in piecemeal fashion as buildings were improved.

River and water-table levels in York

Changes in the levels of the Foss and Ouse and waterlogging of the thick organic build-up have probably been important factors in the history of settlement at York. At the present day the Ouse regularly floods to levels well above many areas occupied in the past (Radley & Simms 1970). Previous work relating to the ancient topography of York and its immediate surroundings has perhaps failed to take account of the great variability in the depth of the build-up in different areas of the town. Fig 40 shows a section through the city from the 'Anglian tower' south-eastwards across the Roman fortress to the River Foss, based on data from various boreholes and excavations. It shows that surface levels and slopes along this line have

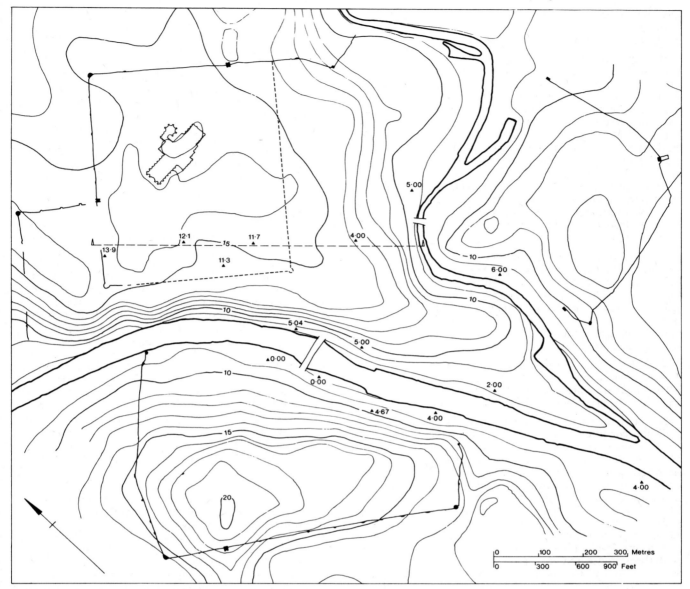

▲ Borehole giving level at which natural ground surface was found (metres O D)

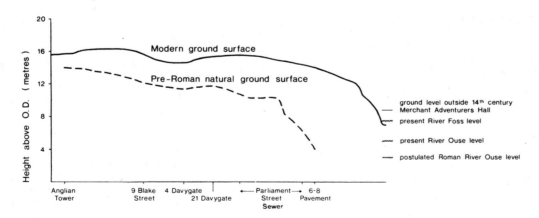

Fig 40   Contour map of York's modern topography, giving the position of the boreholes and of the section (below) which shows the underlying natural topography, based on archaeological and commercial excavations

altered fundamentally in the past nineteen hundred years, with a great deal of the change dating to the Anglo-Scandinavian and early medieval periods.

Borings near to the rivers Foss and Ouse within the boundaries of the city have revealed riverine silts and sands inland of the existing river walls on either side of both rivers. It has been suggested that a cobbled area discovered on the Skeldergate site at approximately 5m OD and some 40m from the existing western bank of the Ouse was a Roman riverside hard (Carver *et al* in press), and borings on the other side of the river suggest that the position of the present 9m contour may be considered to mark the lateral extent of the Roman river in this area. The presence of what appears to have been a well-drained soil below 6m OD on the Skeldergate site suggests a probable maximum river level of 4m OD. Biological evidence from this soil is, however, ambiguous (Kenward & Williams in preparation c).

Indications that the Ouse was once wider have also been discovered on its east bank and it is possible that the stretch of river bank between Lendal Bridge and Ouse Bridge may have sloped more steeply than does the present surface. The section through the city (Fig 40) shows a steeper incline to a much wider Foss basin in Roman times, later deposits tending to have accumulated more in areas adjacent to the river.

The most abundant fish bones in the Church Street Roman sewer were of smelt, an estuarine fish (Wheeler 1976), and with a proposed level below 4m OD the river must have been subject to tidal influence at this period.

Although the silt deposits found in boreholes may merely indicate changing watercourses, it is certain that the medieval period saw considerable narrowing of the river (MacGregor 1975). This evidence can be used to postulate an Anglo-Scandinavian river very much wider than at the present day, at a significantly lower level (possibly between 3 and 4m OD) and in all probability much shallower. Much of the flooding experienced in modern and medieval York is a direct result of the constriction of the river. Until this narrowing occurred there would have been a much smaller rise in river level for a given volume of water. This, together with the presence of more sharply sloping river banks, would mean that flooding would have been less serious than today, the areas inundated probably being unoccupied in any case. Flooding certainly must have occurred in the Vale of York during the Anglo-Scandinavian period and was probably serious in the lower reaches of the Ouse (Palmer 1966; Radley & Simms 1970), although its importance in the city has been overstressed. The very great build-up of deposits adjacent to the river in the Anglo-Scandinavian period (Addyman 1975a) is more likely to have been a result of the organic nature of materials used for buildings and their floor layers than of any rise in water level. The wooden buildings would probably have had a short life-span, and where they have been found on other sites, notably Dublin and in Continental Europe (Leciejewicz 1976), similar massive build-up has been encountered. In fact a vicious circle may have arisen, with sponge-like organic deposits retaining water, giving a damp surface on to which even more material was dumped in an attempt to produce tolerably dry living surfaces.

Climate

The potential of biological investigations of urban settlements in determining past climates has been discussed elsewhere (Addyman *et al* 1976). Climate is obviously a predominant factor in the human environment, and even small changes may be important, particularly through their effect on crops. However, such small-scale changes in climate as have probably occurred during the past two millennia are very difficult to detect. Probably one of the best methods of doing this will be by discovering past changes in the distribution of climate-sensitive insects. Because towns modify climate locally and provide an abundance of protected habitats, urban insects will probably be less useful than the fauna of natural deposits. There is, however, a little evidence from York that Anglo-Scandinavian and early medieval summer temperatures were slightly warmer than at present (Addyman *et al* 1976). This is an exciting area for further research.

Concluding remarks

This paper is largely based on the unpublished work of its authors (reports are in draft). Its preparation has emphasized how little is known about the environment of Anglo-Scandinavian York. Although archaeological and biological studies have already produced a plethora of data, work can only be regarded as in its early stages, and it is producing as many questions as definite answers. Perhaps one of the most valuable aspects of palaeo-environmental studies is in any case to test the conclusions of conventional archaeology and history. It has been beyond the scope of this paper to do more than generalize from the results of the first few years of environmental archaeology at York, a time which has of necessity been as much devoted to developing and testing the techniques of what is largely a new science, as to applying them. The intention has been primarily to define the field and to stimulate thought; the time is not yet ripe for detailed conclusions which will require many years of intensive research.

The excavation of a large area at 16-22 Coppergate has enormous potential but biological investigation of it will be an undertaking of unprecedented proportions. Environmental archaeology is a painstaking and time-consuming science and there is an inevitable conflict between the desire to investigate thoroughly every aspect of a particular site and the need to see a wide range of different material. Comparison of the results of work on the Coppergate and Pavement area with other parts of the Viking-age town, with other contemporaneous towns here and abroad, and with other periods will be both necessary and fascinating. In addition, much work remains to be done on modern plants and animals, particularly on the way their remains become incorporated into deposits comparable with archaeological ones, before the evidence from archaeological sites can be fully evaluated. A full understanding of urban life also depends on a knowledge of rural conditions and in order to obtain this it will be necessary to investigate the plant and animal remains from rural settlements and natural deposits. Environmental archaeology is a new field which has hardly found its identity; at York it clearly has a very great potential.

Acknowledgements

The authors are indebted to John Hood for discussion of the pedological evidence, Marion Berry and Allan Hall for comments on the text, the staff of York Archaeological Trust for their constant cooperation, Jan Donohue for typing drafts, and Tish Kenward for typing the table and for help in revising the text. The help of Richard Hall and Valerie Black in rationalizing the paper has been much appreciated.

Bibliography

Addyman, P V, 1975a   Excavations in York, 1972-1973, First interim report, *Antiq J*, **54**, 200-31
——————, 1975b   York Archaeological Trust work in 1974, reprinted from *Yorkshire Philosoph Soc Annu Rep for 1974*
——————, 1976a   York Archaeological Trust work in 1975, reprinted from *Yorkshire Philosoph Soc Annu Rep for 1975*
——————, 1976b   *Excavations in York 1973-74, Second interim report*
——————, 1977   York Archaeological Trust work in 1976, reprinted from *Yorkshire Philosoph Soc Annu Rep for 1976*
Addyman, P V, & Harrison, M, 1975   6/8 Pavement: Anglo-Saxon and Anglo-Scandinavian deposits, in Addyman 1975a, 218-24
Addyman, P V, Hood, J S R, Kenward, H K, MacGregor, A, & Williams, D, 1976   Palaeoclimate in urban environmental archaeology at York, England; problems and potential, *World Archaeol*, **8**, 220-33
Andersen, H H, Crabb, P J, & Madsen, H J, 1971   *Århus Søndervold*
Anon 1973   *Viking and medieval Dublin*
Arbman, H, 1943   *Birka* **1** *Die Gräber*
Arnold, T (ed), 1882-5   *Symeonis Monachi Opera Omnia*, 2 vols (Rolls Series)
Bailey, R N, & Lang, J T, 1975   The date of the Gosforth sculptures, *Antiquity*, **49**, 290-3
Baker, L G D, 1970   The desert in the north, *Northern Hist*, **5**, 1-11
——————, 1975   Scissors and paste: Corpus Christi, Cambridge, MS 139 again, in *Studies in Church history, Vol II*, 83-123
Barley, M W, 1964   The medieval borough of Torksey: excavations 1960-2, *Antiq J*, **44**, 164-87
Bartley, D D, 1975   Pollen analytical evidence for prehistoric forest clearance in the upland area of Rishworth, West Yorkshire, *New Phytologist*, **74**, 375-81
Bartley, D D, Chambers, C, & Hart-Jones, B, 1976   The vegetational history of parts of south and east Durham, *ibid*, **77**, 437-68
Battiscombe, C F (ed), 1956   *The relics of St Cuthbert*
Beckwith, J, 1972   *Ivory carvings in medieval England*
Benson, G, 1902   Notes on excavations at 25, 26, and 27, High Ousegate, York, *Annu Rep of the Council of the Yorkshire Philosophical Society, 1902* (1903), 64-7
——————, 1906   Notes on an excavation at the corner of Castlegate and Coppergate, *ibid 1906* (1907), 72-6
Bergquist, H, & Lepiksaar, J, 1957   *Animal skeletal remains from medieval Lund*, Archaeology of Lund, **1**
Bersu, G, 1947   The rath in Townland Lissue, Co Antrim, *Ulster J Archaeol*, 3 ser, **10**, 30-58
Biddle, M, 1976   Towns, in Wilson 1976d, 99-150
Binns, A L, 1956   Tenth century carvings from Yorkshire and the Jellinge style, *Universitetet i Bergen Årbok*
Birch, W de Gray (ed), 1892   *Liber Vitae: Register and martyrology of New Minster and Hyde Abbey, Winchester*, Hampshire Record Society
Bishop, S, 1976   Skeldergate: Anglian and Anglo-Scandinavian buildings, in Addyman 1976b, 14
Blindheim, C, 1972   *Kaupang: vikingenes handelsplass*
Blomqvist, R, 1938   Medeltida skor i Lund, *Kulturen*, 189-219
——————, 1942   Kammar fran Lunds Medeltid, *ibid*, 133-62
Brøndsted, J, 1924   *Early English ornament*
Buckland, P C, 1973   Archaeology and environment in the Vale of York, *S Yorkshire Studies in Archaeol and Natur Hist*, **1**, 6-16
——————, 1974   Archaeology and environment in York, *J Archaeol Sci*, **1**, 303-16
Buckland, P C, Greig, J R A, & Kenward, H K, 1974   York: an early medieval site, *Antiquity*, **48**, 25-33
Carver, M O H, 1976   Bishophill: destruction of Roman buildings and Anglo-Scandinavian occupation, in Addyman 1976b, 12
Carver, M O H, Donaghey, S, & Sumpter, A B, in press   *Riverside structures and a well at Skeldergate and buildings at Bishophill, The archaeology of York*, **4**/1 (ed P V Addyman)
Charles-Edwards, T M, 1976   The distinction between land and moveable wealth in Anglo-Saxon England, in Sawyer 1976b, 180-90
Christensen, A E, 1970   Klåstadskipet, *Nicolay*, **8**, 21-4
Clarkson, L A, 1974   The English bark trade, 1660-1830, *Agr Hist Rev*, **22**, 136-52
Cleasby, R, Vigfusson, G, & Craigie, W A, 1962   *An Icelandic-English Dictionary*, 2 edn

Colgrave, B, 1950   The post-Bedan miracles and translations of St Cuthbert, in *The early cultures of north-west Europe (H M Chadwick Memorial Studies)* (eds Sir Cyril Fox and Bruce Dickins), 305-32
Collingwood, W G, 1907a   Some illustrations of the archaeology of the Viking Age in England, *Saga Book of the Viking Society for Northern Research*, **5**, 108-41
——————, 1907b   Anglian and Anglo-Danish sculpture in the North Riding of Yorkshire, *Yorkshire Archaeol J*, **19**, 266-413
——————, 1909   Anglian and Anglo-Danish sculpture at York, *ibid*, **20**, 149-213
——————, 1911   Anglian and Anglo-Danish sculpture in the East Riding, *ibid*, **21**, 254-302
——————, 1914   Anglian and Anglo-Danish sculpture in the West Riding, *ibid*, **23**, 129-299
——————, 1927   *Northumbrian crosses of the pre-Norman Age*
——————, 1929   A cross-fragment at Sutton-on-Derwent, *Yorkshire Archaeol J*, **29**, 238-40
Cowling, G C, 1967   *The history of Easingwold and the Forest of Galtres*
Cox, J C, 1905   *The Royal forests of England*
Cramp, R, 1967   *Anglian and Viking York*, Borthwick Papers, **33**
Craster, E, 1954   The patrimony of St Cuthbert, *Eng Hist Rev*, **49**, 177-99
Crawford, O G S, Röder, J, *et al*, 1955   The quern-quarries of Mayen in the Eifel, *Antiquity*, **29**, 68-76
de Boer, G, 1965   Eastern Yorkshire: the geographical background to early settlement, in *The Fourth Viking Congress* (ed A Small) 197-210
Dolley, R H M, 1966a   *The Hiberno-Norse coins in the British Museum, Sylloge of coins of the British Isles*, **3**
——————, 1966b   New light on the pre-1760 Coney Street (York) find of coins of the Duurstede mint, *Jaarboek voor Munt en Penningkunde*, **52-3**, 1-7
Dunning, G C, 1956   Trade relations between England and the Continent in the late Anglo-Saxon period, in *Dark Age Britain* (ed J D B Harden) 218-33
Dyer, J, & Wenham, P, 1958   Excavations and discoveries in a cellar in Messrs Chas Hart's premises, Feasegate, York, 1956, *Yorkshire Archaeol J*, **39**, 419-25
Ekman, J, 1973   Early medieval Lund—the fauna and landscape, *Archaeol Lundensia*, **5**
Ellis, S E, 1969   The petrography and provenance of Anglo-Saxon and medieval English honestones, with notes on some other hones, *Bull Brit Mus (Natur Hist) Mineralogy*, **2**, 135-87
Faull, M L, 1974   Roman and Anglian settlement patterns in Yorkshire, *Northern Hist*, **9**, 1-25
Fife, M G, & Walls, P J, 1973   *The River Foss from Yearsley village to York: its history and natural history*
Geijer, A, 1938   *Birka* **3** *Die Textilfunde aus den Gräbern*
Gerarde, J, 1636   *The Herball or Generall Historie of Plantes*, enlarged and amended by Thomas Johnson, citizen and apothecarye of London
Godwin, H, 1967a   The ancient cultivation of hemp, *Antiquity*, **41**, 42-8, 137-8
——————, 1967b   Pollen-analytic evidence for the cultivation of *Cannabis* in England, *Review of Palaeobotany and Palynology*, **4**, 71-80
——————, 1975   *The history of the British flora. A factual basis for phytogeography*, 2 edn
Godwin, H, & Bachem, K, 1959   Appendix III. Plant material, in Richardson 1959, 109-13
Grigson, G, 1958   *The Englishman's flora*
Groenman-van Waateringe, W, & Velt, L M, 1975   Schuhmode im Späten Mittelalter, Funde und Abbildungen, *Zeitschrift für Archäologie des Mittelalters*, **3**, 95-119
Grove, L R A, 1939   An Anglo-Saxon loom-weight from York Castle, *Yorkshire Archaeol J*, **34**, 113
——————, 1940   A Viking bone trial piece from York Castle, *Antiq J*, **20**, 285-7
Guillou, A, 1974   Production and profits in the Byzantine province of Italy (tenth to eleventh centuries): an expanding society, *Dumbarton Oaks Papers*, **28**, 89-109
——————, 1976   La Soie du Katapénat d'Italie, *Travaux et Mémoires*, **6**, 69-84

Hald, M, 1972   *Primitive shoes,* Publs of the National Museum of Denmark, Archaeol Hist Ser 1, **13**

Hall, R A, 1975   Keyhole archaeology: St Mary Castlegate, *Interim,* **3** (1), 18-28

————, 1976a   *The Viking kingdom of York*

————, 1976b   Coppergate: watching briefs, in Addyman 1976b, 15

Hall, R A, & Kenward, H K, 1976   Biological evidence for the usage of Roman riverside warehouses at York, *Britannia,* **7,** 274-6

Hamilton, J R C, 1956   *Excavations at Jarlshof, Shetland*

————, 1962   Brochs and the broch builders, in *The northern isles* (ed F T Wainwright), 53-90

Hart, C R, 1975   *The early charters of northern England and the north midlands*

Haverfield, F J, & Greenwell, W, 1899   *A catalogue of the sculptured and inscribed stones in the Cathedral Library, Durham*

Heighway, C M (ed), 1972   *The erosion of history*

Hencken, H O'N, 1950   Lagore Crannog: an Irish royal residence of the 7th to 10th centuries AD, *Proc Roy Ir Acad,* **53C,** 1-247

Hennessy, W M (ed), 1866   *Chronicum Scotorum*

———— (ed), 1887   *Annals of Ulster*

Henry, F, 1967   *Irish art during the Viking invasions*

————, 1970   *Irish art in the Romanesque period*

Hist Dun Eccl   *Historia Dunelmensis Ecclesiae,* in Arnold i, 3-135

Historia   *Historia de Sancto Cuthberto,* in Arnold i, 196-214

Hodges, H, 1964   *Artifacts*

Hohler, C E, 1975   Some service books of the late Saxon church, in *Tenth century studies* (ed D Parsons), 60-83, 217-27

Holdsworth, J, forthcoming   *Selected ceramic groups from York c 650-1780, The archaeology of York,* **16** (ed P V Addyman)

Holmqvist, W (ed), 1961   *Excavations at Helgö* I

———— (ed), 1970   *Excavations at Helgö* III

Holmqvist, W, & Arrhenius, B (eds), 1964   *Excavations at Helgö* II

Howarth, E, 1899   *Catalogue of the Bateman collection of antiquities in the Sheffield public museum*

Hughes, G B, 1953   *Living crafts*

Hunter Blair, P, 1963   Some observations on the *Historia Regum* attributed to Symeon of Durham, in *Celt and Saxon* (ed N K Chadwick) 63-118

Hurst, J G, 1958   Saxo-Norman pottery in East Anglia, *Proc Cambridge Antiq Soc,* **51,** 37-65

————, 1969a   The pottery, in Excavations at the Saxon monastic sites of Wearmouth and Jarrow, Co Durham: an interim report (R Cramp), *Medieval Archaeol,* **13,** 59-64

———— (ed), 1969b   Red painted and glazed pottery in western Europe from the eighth to the twelfth century, *Medieval Archaeol,* **13,** 93-147

Interim   Bulletin of York Archaeological Trust (quarterly)

Jellema, D, 1955   Frisian trade in the Dark Ages, *Speculum,* **30,** 15-36

Jensen, G F, 1972   *Scandinavian settlement names in Yorkshire*

————, 1975   The Vikings in England: a review, in *Anglo-Saxon England, Vol 4* (ed P Clemoes), 181-206

Jones, G, 1968   *A history of the Vikings*

Jope, E M, 1956   The tinning of iron spurs: a continuous practice from the tenth to the seventeenth century, *Oxoniensia,* **21,** 35-42

Kay, Q O N, 1971   Biological flora of the British Isles. *Anthemis cotula* L., *J Ecol,* **59,** 623-6

Kendrick, T D, 1935   Note on an ivory implement from Bramham, Yorks, *Yorkshire Archaeol J,* **32,** 339-40

————, 1938   *Anglo-Saxon art to AD 900* (reprint 1972)

————, 1949   *Late Saxon and Viking art*

————, 1968   *A history of the Vikings*

Kenward, H K, 1975a   The biological and archaeological implications of the beetle *Aglenus brunneus* (Gyllenhal) in ancient faunas, *J Archaeol Sci,* **2,** 63-9

————, 1975b   Pitfalls in the environmental interpretation of insect death assemblages, *ibid,* **2,** 85-94

————, 1976a   Reconstructing ancient ecological conditions from insect remains; some problems and an experimental approach, *Ecological Entomology,* **1,** 7-17

————, 1976b   Further archaeological records of *Aglenus brunneus* (Gyll.) in Britain and Ireland, including confirmation of its presence in the Roman period, *J Archaeol Sci,* **3,** 275-7

————, in press a   *The analysis of archaeological insect faunas: a new approach, The archaeology of York,* **19**/1 (ed P V Addyman)

————, in press b   A note on the insect remains from column 3, sample 4, in Excavations in Sewer Lane, Hull (P Armstrong), *E Riding Archaeol,* **3** (Hull Old Town Report Ser 1)

Kenward, H K, & Williams, D, in press   *Biological evidence for Roman grain stores at 39-41 Coney Street, The archaeology of York,* **14**/2 (ed P V Addyman)

————, in preparation a   *Biological evidence from the Anglo-Scandinavian site at 6-8 Pavement, ibid*

————, in preparation b   *A medieval moss-lined pit from Skeldergate, York, ibid*

————, in preparation c   *Biological evidence from the Roman levels at Skeldergate, ibid*

Ker, N R, 1943   Aldred the scribe, *Essays and Studies,* **28,** 7-12

————, 1957   *Catalogue of manuscripts containing Anglo-Saxon*

King, A, 1969   *A study of early settlement in Upper Ribblesdale and adjacent uplands,* MA dissertation, Univ Liverpool

————, 1970   *Early Pennine settlement*

King, A, & Walker, W H, 1966   *Yorkshire Archaeol J,* **41,** 559-60

King, J E, 1964   *Seals of the world*

Kloet, G S, & Hincks, W D, 1977   *A check list of British insects, Part 3, Coleoptera and Strepsiptera* (revised R D Pope) 2 edn

Knowles, W H, 1905   Sockburn Church, *Trans Architect Archaeol Soc Durham Northumberland,* **5,** 99-120

Lang, J T, 1971   The Castledermot Hogback, *J Roy Soc Antiq Ir,* **101,** 154-8

————, 1973   Some late pre-Conquest crosses in Ryedale, Yorkshire: a reappraisal, *J Brit Archaeol Ass,* **36,** 16-25

————,1976   Sigurd and Weland in pre-Conquest carving from northern England, *Yorkshire Archaeol J,* **48,** 83-94

————, 1977   The sculptors of the Nunburnholme Cross, *Archaeol J,* **133,** 75-94

Leciejewicz, L, 1976   Medieval archaeology in Poland; current problems and research methods, *Medieval Archaeol,* **20,** 1-15

Le Patourel, H E J, 1965   The pottery, in Pontefract Priory excavations 1957-1961 (C V Bellamy), *Publ Thoresby Soc,* **49,** 106-19

Liebermann, F (ed), 1889   *Die Heiligen Englands*

Long, C D, 1975   Excavations in the medieval city of Trondheim, Norway, *Medieval Archaeol,* **19,** 1-32

Lyon, C S S, 1957   A reappraisal of the sceatta and styca coinage of Northumbria, *Brit Numis J,* **8,** 227-42

MacGregor, A, 1975   The old warehouse site, Skeldergate, in Addyman 1975a, 225-7

————, 1976   Bone skates: a review of the evidence, *Archaeol J,* **133,** 57-74

————,forthcoming   *Anglo-Scandinavian finds from Lloyds Bank, Pavement, and elsewhere, The archaeology of York,* **17** (ed P V Addyman)

Miller, N, Williams, D, & Kenward, H K, in press   Biological evidence from Mytongate, Hull, *E Riding Archaeol* (Hull Old Town Report ser)

Mossop, H R, 1970   *The Lincoln mint c 890-1279*

Mynors, R A B, 1939   *Durham Cathedral manuscripts to the end of the twelfth century*

Nørlund, P, 1948   *Trelleborg*

Oldfield, F, 1963   Pollen analysis and man's role in the ecological history of the south-east Lake District, *Geografiska Annaler,* **45,** 23-40

O'Neil, B H St J, 1939   Excavations at York Castle, 1935, *Antiq J,* **19,** 85-9

Ó Ríordáin, A B, 1971   Excavations at High Street and Winetavern Street, Dublin, *Medieval Archaeol,* **15,** 73-85

————, 1976   The High Street excavations, in *Proceedings of the Seventh Viking Congress* (eds B Almqvist & D Greene) 135-40

Ormer-Cooper, J, & Tottenham, C E, 1934   Coleoptera taken in the air at Wicken Fen, *Entomologist's Monthly Mag,* **70,** 231-4

Page, W, 1907   *A history of Yorkshire. The Victoria history of the counties of England*

Palliser, D, & Hall, R A, 1975   Keyhole archaeology, *Interim,* **2** (3), 32-5

Palmer, J, 1966   Landforms, drainage and settlement in the Vale of York, in *Geography as human ecology* (eds S R Eyre & G R J Jones), 91-121

Pattison, I R, 1973   The Nunburnholme Cross and Anglo-Danish sculpture in York, *Archaeologia,* **104,** 209-34

Pennington, W, 1970   Vegetational history in the north-west of England: a regional synthesis, in *Studies in the vegetational history of the British Isles* (eds D Walker & R G West), 41-79

Pertz, G H (ed), 1866   *Monumenta Germaniae Historica (Scriptorum), Vol 19*

Petersen, J, 1928   *Vikingetidens Smykker*

Phillips, D, 1975   Excavations at York Minster 1967-73, *Annu Rep Friends of York Minster,* **46,** 19-27

Pirie, E J E, 1975   *Coins in Yorkshire collections, Sylloge of coins of the British Isles,* **21**

Plummer, C, 1896   *Venerabilis Bædae Opera Historica*

Plummer, C, & Earle, J (eds), 1965   *Two Saxon chronicles parallel*

Rackham, D J, in preparation   *Animal remains from four early medieval sites in York, The archaeology of York* (ed P V Addyman)

Rackham, O, 1976   *Trees and woodland in the British landscape*

Radley, J, 1971   Economic aspects of Anglo-Danish York, *Medieval Archaeol,* **15,** 37-57

————, 1972   Excavations in the defence of the city of York: an early medieval stone tower and the successive earth ramparts, *Yorkshire Archaeol J,* **44,** 38-64

————, 1974   The prehistory of the Vale of York, *ibid,* **46,** 10-22

Radley, J, & Simms, C, 1970   *Yorkshire flooding: some effects on man and nature*

Raine, A, 1955   *Medieval York*

Raine, J, 1879   *The historians of the Church of York and its Archbishops* I

Ramm, H G, 1971   The end of Roman York, in *Soldier and civilian in Roman Yorkshire* (ed R M Butler), 179-99

———, 1972   The growth and development of the city to the Norman Conquest, in *The noble city of York* (ed A Stacpoole), 225-54

———, 1976   The Church of St Mary Bishophill Senior, York: excavations 1964, *Yorkshire Archaeol J*, **48**, 35-68

RCHMY 1   *An inventory of the historical monuments in the city of York, Vol 1, Eburacum. Roman York*, Royal Commission on Historical Monuments, England

RCHMY 4   *An inventory of the historical monuments in the city of York, Vol 4, Outside the city walls east of the Ouse, ibid*

Reed, R, 1972   *Ancient skins, parchments and leathers*

Reichstein, H, 1969   Untersuchungen an Geweihresten des Rothirsches . . ., in *Ausgrabungen in Haithabu*, **2** (ed K Schietzel), 57-71

Reichstein, H, & Tiessen, M, 1974   Untersuchungen an Tierknochen-funden, 1963-1964, *ibid*, **7**

Richardson, K M, 1959   Excavations in Hungate, York, *Archaeol J*, **116**, 51-114

Robertson, A J (ed), 1956   *Anglo-Saxon charters*, 2 edn

Robinson, M, & Hubbard, R N L, 1977   The transport of pollen in the bracts of hulled cereals, *J Archaeol Sci*, **4**, 197-9

Roes, A, 1965   *Vondsten van Dorestad*, Archaeologia Traiectina, **7**

Rollason, D W, forthcoming   Lists of Saints' resting places in Anglo-Saxon England, in *Anglo-Saxon England* (ed P Clemoes)

Russel, J, 1939   English medieval leatherwork, *Archaeol J*, **96**, 132-41

Ryder, M L, 1963   Remains derived from skin, in *Science in archaeology* (eds D Brothwell & E Higgs), 539-54

———, 1970   The animal remains from Petergate, York 1957-58, *Yorkshire Archaeol J*, **42**, 418-28

———, in press   Animal fibres and fleece types, in *Anglo-Scandinavian finds from Lloyds Bank, Pavement, and elsewhere* (A MacGregor), *The archaeology of York*, **17** (ed P V Addyman)

Salzman, L F, 1964   *English industries of the Middle Ages*

Sawyer, P H, 1968   *Anglo-Saxon charters: an annotated list and bibliography*, Royal Historical Society Guides and Handbooks, **8**

———, 1971   *The age of the Vikings*, 2 edn

———, 1974   Anglo-Saxon settlement: the documentary evidence, in *Anglo-Saxon settlement and landscape* (ed T Rowley) 108-19

———, 1975   The charters of Burton Abbey and the unification of England, *Northern Hist*, **10**, 28-39

———, 1976a   Early medieval English settlement, in Sawyer 1976b, 1-7

——— (ed), 1976b   *Medieval settlement: continuity and change*

Schietzel, K, 1970   Das archäologische Fundmaterial 1 (1963-1964), *Ausgrabungen in Haithabu*, **4**

Schove, D J, 1950   Visions in north-west Europe (AD 400-600) and dated auroral displays, *J Brit Archaeol Ass* 3 ser, **13**, 34-49

Seaward, M R D, & Williams, D, 1976   An interpretation of mosses found in recent archaeological excavations, *J Archaeol Sci*, **3**, 173-7

Shetelig, H (ed), 1940   *Viking antiquities in Great Britain and Ireland, Vol 4, Viking antiquities in England*

——— (ed), 1944   Smykker av Jet i Norske Vikingefunn, *Bergens Museums Årbok*, 1-14

——— (ed), 1948   The Norse style of ornamentation in the Viking settlements, *Acta Archaeologica*, **19**, 69-113

——— (ed), 1954   *Viking antiquities in Great Britain and Ireland, Part 6*

Skjølsvold, A, 1961   *Klebersteinindustrien i Vikingetiden*

Smith, A H, 1937   The place names of the East Riding of Yorkshire, *English Place-Name Society*, **14**

Smith, R A, 1902   Anglo-Saxon remains, in *The Victoria history of the county of Northampton, Vol 1* (eds W Ryland, D Adkins, & R M Serjeantson), 223-56

———, 1909   Anglo-Saxon remains, in *The Victoria history of London, Vol 1* (ed W Page), 147-70

Smyth, A P, 1975   *Scandinavian York and Dublin I*

———, 1977   *Scandinavian kings in the British Isles*, 850-80

———, 1978   *Scandinavian York and Dublin II*

Stead, I M L, 1958   Excavations at the south corner tower of the Roman fortress at York 1956, *Yorkshire Archaeol J*, **39**, 515-38

———, 1968   An excavation at King's Square, York, 1957, *ibid*, **42**, 151-64

Stenton, F M, 1970   *Preparatory to Anglo-Saxon England* (ed D M Stenton)

———, 1971   *Anglo-Saxon England*, 3 edn

Thompson, A H, 1923   *Liber Vitae Ecclesiae Dunelmensis*, Surtees Soc, **136**

———, 1935   Northumbrian monasticism, in *Bede, his life, times, and writings* (ed A H Thompson), 60-101

Thompson, A H, and Lindelöf, U (eds), 1927   *Rituale Ecclesiae Dunelmensis*, Surtees Soc, **140**

Warren, F E (ed), 1883   *The Leofric Missal*

Waterman, D M, 1959   Late Saxon, Viking and early medieval finds from York, *Archaeologia*, **97**, 59-105

Webster, L, & Cherry, J, 1972   Medieval Britain in 1971, *Medieval Archaeol*, **16**, 147-212

Wenham, L P, 1968   Discoveries in King's Square, York, 1963, *Yorkshire Archaeol J*, **42**, 165-8

———, 1972   Excavations in Low Petergate, York, 1957-58, *ibid*, **44**, 65-113

Wheeler, A, 1976   Fishes, in *The environmental evidence from the Church Street Roman sewer system, The archaeology of York*, **14**/1 (ed P V Addyman), 33-4

Whitelock, D (ed), 1955   *English historical documents, Vol 1, c 500-1042*

———, 1959   The dealings of the kings of England with Northumbria in the tenth and eleventh centuries, in *The Anglo-Saxons: studies . . . presented to Bruce Dickins* (ed P Clemoes), 70-88

——— (ed & trans), 1961   *The Anglo-Saxon Chronicle* (with D C Douglas & S I Tucker)

———, 1965   On the commencement of the year in the Saxon chronicles, in Plummer & Earle 1965

William of Malmesbury   Hamilton, N E S A (ed), 1870. *Gesta Pontificum Willelmi Malmesbiriensis Monachi, De Gestis Pontificum Anglorum*

Wilson, D M, 1965   Two 10th-century bronze objects, *Medieval Archaeol*, **9**, 154-6

———, 1968a   Anglo-Saxon carpenters' tools, in *Studien zur europäischen Vor- und Frühgeschichte* (eds M Claus *et al*), 143-50

———, 1968b   Archaeological evidence for the Viking settlements and raids in England, *Frühmittelalterliche Studien*, **2**, 291-304

Wilson, D M, 1976a   The Scandinavian settlement in the north and west of the British Isles—an archaeological point of view, *Trans Roy Hist Soc*, **26**, 95-113

———, 1976b   The Scandinavians in England, in Wilson 1976d, 393-403

———, 1976c   Craft and industry, in Wilson 1976d, 253-281

——— (ed), 1976d   *The archaeology of Anglo-Saxon England*

Wilson, D M, & Hurst, D G, 1963   Medieval Britain in 1961, *Medieval Archaeol*, **6-7**, 306-49

Wilson, D M, & Klindt-Jensen, O, 1966   *Viking art*

Wormald, F (ed) 1934   *English Kalendars before AD 1100*, Henry Bradshaw Soc, **72**

——— (ed), 1939   *English Benedictine Kalendars after AD 1100, vol i, ibid*, **77**